THE MAKING OF A UNIVERSITY
THE PATH TO HIGHER EDUCATION
IN HUDDERSFIELD

HUDDERSFIELD TECHNICAL SCHOOL, OPENED Saturday, July 7th, 1883, by His Grace the DUKE of SOMERSET, K.G.

The Making of a University

The Path to Higher Education in Huddersfield

John O'Connell

University of
HUDDERSFIELD
Press

Published by University of Huddersfield Press

University of Huddersfield Press
The University of Huddersfield
Queensgate
Huddersfield HD1 3DH
Email enquiries university.press@hud.ac.uk

First published 2016
Text © The Author
Images © as attributed
Edited by John Lancaster

Every effort has been made to locate copyright holders of materials included and to obtain permission for their publication.

The publisher is not responsible for the continued existence and accuracy of websites referenced in the text.

All rights reserved. No part of this book may be reproduced in any form or by any means without prior permission from the publisher.

A CIP catalogue record for this book is available from the British Library.

ISBN 978-1-86218-054-3

Page Layout by Highlight Type Bureau, Ltd., Bradford BD19 4TQ
Printed by The Amadeus Press, Cleckheaton BD19 4TQ

Notes on the Plates
Plates 8, 15, 16, 17, 23, 24, 25, 26, 29, 33 and 65 are reproduced with the kind agreement of Kirklees Libraries. Plate 13 is reproduced from an "out of copyright" image in the Illustrated London News, 1880. Plate 19 is reproduced from an "out of copyright" Ordnance Survey Map. Plates 32 and 34 are drawings created by Anna Todd. Plates 38 and 59 are reproduced with the kind permission of the Huddersfield Examiner. All other plates are drawn from the collections of the University of Huddersfield Archives and Special Collections.

Acknowledgments
The editor wishes to place on record his particular thanks to Emeritus Professor Brendan Evans; Professor Tim Thornton, Deputy Vice-Chancellor; Sue White, Director of Computing & Library Services; Hilary Haigh, Honorary Archivist; Christine Collier, Ann West, John Ramsdin, Tony Mears, Tracey Buxton, Lindsay Ince and Brian Haigh - all of the University of Huddersfield; Angela Lawless of Highlight Type Bureau; Stephen Carter of the Huddersfield Examiner; Anna Todd, artist; Richard Cook and Richard Lambert of The Amadeus Press; and the staff of Kirklees Local Studies Library.

Contents

List of Plates ix
List of Colour Plates xi
Foreword xii
Preface xiii

Part I: From Mechanics' Institution to Polytechnic, 1841-1970
1. The Founding Fathers, 1841-54 1
2. The Transition to Technical School, 1854-83 13
3. The First Age of Technical Education, 1884-1914: 25
    a) *The Road to Municipalisation, 1884-1903;*
    b) *The Pre-War Municipal Technical College, 1903-14.*
4. War and Peace, 1914-46: 41
    a) *The First World War and its Aftermath, 1914-24;*
    b) *Between the Wars, 1918-39;*
    c) *The Second World War, 1939-46.*
5. The Scott Era, 1946-70: 55
    a) *A Decade of Uncertainty, 1946-56;*
    b) *The Halting Progression to Polytechnic Status, 1956-70.*

Part II: The Polytechnic of Huddersfield, 1970-1992
6. The Establishment of the Polytechnic and the Merger
   with Holly Bank, 1970-74: 73
    a) *The Establishment of the Polytechnic, 1970-72;*
    b) *The Merger with Holly Bank and Departments*
        in Flux, 1972-74.
7. Adjusting to Kirklees, and the Crisis of 1979-81 (1974-81): 85
    a) *Adjusting to Kirklees, 1974-79;*
    b) *Mounting Troubles and the Crisis of 1979-81.*
8. Roles, Relationships and the Road to Independence, 1982-89: 107
    a) *Roles and Relationships, 1982-84;*
    b) *Evolution to Independence, 1985-89.*
9. The Higher Education Corporation: Polytechnic to University, 1989-92: 135
    a) *Establishment of the Corporation, 1989-91;*
    b) *"A Happy and Successful Year", 1991-92.*

Postscript 155

Appendix 157

Index 159

List of Abbreviations

AC Bd	Academic Board
AC	Academic Board
AR	Annual Report
CBH	County Borough of Huddersfield
CNAA	Council for National Academic Awards
DipFE	Diploma in Further Education
DNB	Dictionary of National Biography
DR	Director's Report
FE S-C	Further Education Sub Committee
GC	Governing Council
GPC	General Purposes Committee
Govs Mins	Governors Minutes
HCBC	Huddersfield County Borough Council
HCOT	Huddersfield College of Technology
HDE	Huddersfield Daily Examiner
HMSO	Her Majesty's Stationery Office
KMC	Kirklees Metropolitan Council
PP	Parliamentary Papers
PR	Principal's Report
Proc Counc	Proceedings of Council
S-C	Sub Committee
Tech & FE Sub-Comm.	Technical & Further Education Sub Committee
Tech Coll Sub-Comm	Technical College Sub Committee
UHA*	University of Huddersfield Archive
WYASK	West Yorkshire Archive Service, Kirklees

Its online catalogue and a guide to the collections are available at www.heritagequay.org

Note by the Author on the University Motto "Trivium Quadrivium"

Trivium and Quadrivium were the curricula taught in universities from the 12th century.
Trivium = grammar, logic, rhetoric
Quadrivium = arithmetic, geometry, astronomy and music theory
Together these were known as the seven liberal arts.

List of Plates

1. Frederic Schwann
2. Nelson's Buildings
3. Nelson's Buildings: rental agreement extract from the Minute Book of 1841 recording the secretary's agreement with Mr Nelson for the lease of "the unoccupied room" on the first floor of the building at the junction of New Street and Cloth Hall Street "at the reduced rent of £10"
4. Wellington Buildings, Queen Street
5. Edmund Eastwood
6. G D Tomlinson
7. Mechanics' Institution, Northumberland Street, occupied by the College between 1861 and 1883
8. Frank Curzon, Secretary, Mechanics' Institution, 1854-62
9. George Jarmain: teacher of Chemistry
10. Alderman John Fligg Brigg
11. Huddersfield Technical School in the 1880s
12. Sir John William Ramsden
13. The Marquess of Ripon
14. Sir Joseph Crosland
15. Technical School, Huddersfield
16. Professor Michael Sadler
17. Ramsden Building with its 1900s extension
18. Museum Room, Huddersfield Technical School
19. Ordnance Survey map of Technical College and its surrounds
20. Huddersfield Technical School
21. Principal J F Hudson
22. Sir John Arthur Brooke
23. Sir Thomas Brooke
24. Tolson Museum
25. Student on a loom
26. Alderman Albert Hirst
27. Dr J W Whitaker
28. Chemistry Building, Queen Street South, (now Queensgate) - opened in 1940
29. Prospectus title page 1936/37
30. Dr W E Scott
31. Chemistry students in the 1940s
32. Anthony Crosland, Secretary of State for Education and Science, 1965-67
33. Alderman John L Dawson
34. Dr Donald Coggan, Archbishop of York
35. Queen Street South c1960 looking south and showing (on the left) the Chemistry Building and beyond it, the original Technical College building of 1883
36. Students' Union
37. Textiles Department. This building is located at the corner of Queen Street South (now Queensgate) and Princess Street, and opposite the 1883 building
38. College facility
39. Central Services Building and Tower
40. Polytechnic entrance. The Textile Department Tower is on the left and Z block is on the right
41. Mrs Margaret Thatcher, Alderman Douglas Sissons and Mr Kenneth J Durrands at the Polytechnic's designation ceremony, 23 April 1971
42. Mrs Margaret Thatcher at the designation ceremony, 23 April 1971
43. A view of the Central Services Building
44. Architect's model of the Central Services Building
45. Ramsden Building in the 1970s
46. Map of the Polytechnic campus in 1975
47. Queensgate Studios, Market Hall – a town centre location for part of the School of Art in the 1970s
48. Co-operative Building – a temporary location for academic activity

49. Queen Street Annexe – a temporary location for part of the School of Music and the Department of Marketing and Accounting
50. Music Department, gathered together in Huddersfield Town Hall
51. Trinity Hall – student accommodation
52. Trinity Hall – student accommodation
53. Trinity Hall – student accommodation
54. Bankfield House – student accommodation
55. Bankfield House – student accommodation
56. Bay Hall – student accommodation
57. Warrenfield – student accommodation
58. 22 Greenhead Road – student accommodation
59. Councillor C I Mernagh
60. Mr K J Durrands, Rector of Huddersfield Polytechnic
61. Polytechnic and Town Centre
62. An architect's model of the Central Services Building
63. View of the Polytechnic campus
64. Sir Harold Wilson, Rector Kenneth J Durrands and Councillor John Mernagh at the opening of the 'Firth Street Building', May 1983
65. Ramsden Building interior
66. St Paul's interior view
67. Harold Wilson on a visit to the Polytechnic
68. Harold Wilson at the Polytechnic – a study in musical appreciation. The author is second from the left.
69. St Paul's Hall
70. Queensgate Campus temporary building
71. Engineering Tower and Z Block. Z Block is so named because it is one arm of a covered walkway linking the Chemistry building with the Central Services Building
72. Catering Building
73. Catering Building
74. Workshop Block
75. Workshop Block
76. Warrenfield – student accommodation
77. Z Block
78. Longley Park Student Residence site
79. Milton Building entrance
80. Library Information Desk
81. Moving the Library
82. Mr Reg Cross, OBE
83. Z Block
84. Music Block
85. Great Hall and St Paul's
86. Sports Hall
87. Catering Annexe Building
88. St. Paul's Hall and the 1940 building; a view across the Queensgate ring road
89. The ubiquitous Castle Hill
90. 1883 building; a view across the Queensgate ring road
91. A view of the Polytechnic
92. Huddersfield roofscape
93. An academic procession
94. University Central Services Building. An artist's impression
95. Professor John O'Connell

List of Colour Plates

Frontispiece Huddersfield Technical School, 1883
I   Ramsden Building
II   Architectural detail, Ramsden Building
III   St Paul's
IV   St Paul's interior
V   Architectural detail, Ramsden Building
VI   Queen Street South Building
VII   Central Services Building
VIII   Letters Patent of the Polytechnic
IX   Coat of Arms of the Polytechnic
X   Architectural detail, St Paul's

Foreword

THE MAKING OF A UNIVERSITY: THE PATH TO HIGHER EDUCATION IN HUDDERSFIELD

This book is a record of the development of an institution with a remarkable history. Its foundations go back to the early part of the nineteenth century when the local Huddersfield community decided it wanted a place of learning to promote the education of the working classes. The first attempt in 1825 failed after a few years but there was an abiding vision and a second initiative succeeded beyond all expectations. In the intervening years we have seen its development encompassing a mechanics' institution, a female educational institute, a college of technology, a polytechnic and a number of other bodies to become the burgeoning centre of learning it is today. Indeed its mission is as strong now as it was when a mechanics' institute delivered educational opportunity to the local populace.

The author, the late John O'Connell, a former Professor of History at the University has demonstrated a profound knowledge of the subject, drawing on a much larger body of his work which resides in the University Archive.

Whilst in one sense the University of Huddersfield can be called a post-1992 university, in another sense it is a venerable institution with a history that ranks alongside civic universities with apparently older traditions.

The University and its precursors have done much to contribute to the Kirklees area in terms of its local community, its economy and its society and there are many alumni who have developed substantial roles upon graduation. The University is a diverse community which itself reflects the rich and varied traditions and cultures of the region and it is a centre of excellence in a number of disciplines.

I have the privilege of being the University's fourth Vice Chancellor. I obtained my first degree here as well as a PhD and a DSc and in the following years I have seen the University progress and thrive.

Professor Robert Anthony Cryan CBE DL FREng
Vice-Chancellor

Preface

This book has been long in gestation and is the outcome of much compression. On and off, I have been writing about the pre-history of the University of Huddersfield for 20 years. In June 1991, celebrating the 150th anniversary of the institution's foundation, the then Polytechnic of Huddersfield published a brief history I had written, illustrated with line drawings of all the buildings the institution had occupied since the beginnings, under the title, *The Polytechnic of Hudderfield: 150 years of achievement*. Then, in 1992, I contributed a chapter entitled 'From Mechanics' Institution to Polytechnic: Further and Higher Education in Huddersfield, 1841-1970', to an illustrated volume published by Kirklees Cultural Services, *Huddersfield a Most Handsome Town: Aspects of the history and culture of a West Yorkshire town*, edited by E A Hilary Haigh. Thereafter I extended my research and by 1998 had written a manuscript which took the history of the college to the end of 1995. Possibility of a publication was discussed, and, in three stages of contraction, during 1999, I produced the present version, as one which was manageable in size and coherent in theme, in that, consistently with its title, it ends with the establishment of the University, in 1992.

I am indebted to many friends and former colleagues who, though to some it may be a distant memory, have answered my questions or made helpful comments on my scripts. It is not "needless to say" that I alone am responsible for errors and shortcomings that remain.

For her ready co-operation in providing access to the University's records, I thank Mrs Hilary Haigh, to whom I am further indebted for her work in the production of the final forms of the typescript and printed versions, and, with Mr Brian Haigh, for assembling the illustrations; for access to records in their care, I thank the staff of the West Yorkshire Archives Service, Kirklees, and of the Tolson Memorial Museum.

I am grateful for the interest shown in my work and the support given to me by the Vice-Chancellor, Professor Bob Cryan, by his predecessor Vice-Chancellor, Professor John Tarrant, and his sometime Deputy Vice-Chancellor, Professor Fen Arthur, and equally so for that given by the Vice-Chancellor for the academic year 1994-5, Sir William Taylor, Kt., CBE.

My heaviest debt I owe to Professor Brendan Evans, formerly Pro Vice-Chancellor for Academic Affairs, who was my Departmental colleague for more than twenty years, and who has given me unfailing support and shown infinite patience through many delays. To his support I also owe thanks for the expert help I have received in the production of typescripts, through several stages, from Mrs Melanie Saville, Mrs Audrey Dobson, Mrs Suzanne Scott, Mrs Susan Racher and Mrs Ann West, and from the anonymous but highly-efficient members of the University's erstwhile typing pool; I thank them for their work.

Producing this volume has been a volcanic experience: long periods of quiescence have been punctuated by eruptions of activity. For the recovery of the script from what seemed final burial I am grateful to Professor John Lancaster, former Director of Computing and Library Services, who made publication possible.

John O'Connell

PART I

From Mechanics' Institution to Polytechnic
1841-1970

CHAPTER 1

I. Ramsden Building

CHAPTER 1

THE FOUNDING FATHERS, 1841-54

An intended mechanics' institute was founded in Huddersfield in 1825. The 'leading and primary objects' of this Huddersfield Scientific and Mechanic Institute were 'the instruction of mechanics and tradesmen in the scientific principles on which their operations chiefly depend, and to point out their practical application in the various arts of life'. These aims were to be achieved through 'the circulation of a well-selected collection of Books', by lectures on 'particularly practical Mechanics and Chemistry', by exhibitions of mechanical models and chemical apparatus, 'and by having classes for instruction in the higher branches of Arithmetic, Mathematics, etc.'[1] As its first annual report claimed, 'the Institution ... was ... established under highly favourable auspices': it was generously supported by donors, headed by Sir John Ramsden, a leading Whig, who was the near-monopolist landowner in Huddersfield, and was Patron of the Institute, and an impressive number of subscribers. Its list of lecturers included John Dalton, the famous chemist, who was a professor in Manchester, and its library - which its 'Directors' considered 'by far the most valuable feature of the Institution' - had 709 volumes at the time of the second annual report, in June 1827. But the Institute foundered, partly because its bankers failed in the financial crisis of 1826, 'a shock felt throughout the commercial world'.[2] Though it lingered on into the early 1830s, it then changed its character, and was re-founded as the Huddersfield Philosophical Society, whose 'Rules' compared closely with its own.[3]

This Huddersfield institute was one of more than twenty founded in the same year in Lancashire and Yorkshire towns, mainly in the Pennine area, and of which the first and largest were those in Manchester and Leeds.[4] They were part of a national educational movement that followed the foundation of the London Mechanics' Institute, late in 1823, in which foundation the most prominent figures were Henry Brougham and George Birkbeck.[*] The London Institute itself followed the examples recently set by the Edinburgh School of Arts and the Mechanics' Institution in Glasgow, the generally-accepted birthplace of the mechanics' institute movement. Brougham, a Scottish lawyer prominent in national politics on the radical wing of the Whig party, and a future Lord Chancellor, was already an established champion of 'education for the lower orders' when his pamphlet, *Practical Observations upon the Education of the People, Addressed to the Working Classes and their Employers*, was published in January 1825. For Brougham, mechanics' institutes were 'not merely seminaries for teaching mechanics the principles of natural and mechanical sciences, but schools where the working classes generally may learn those branches of knowledge which they cannot master by private reading ...'[5] The Broughamites were disparaged by some as 'the knowledge school': their monuments were the mechanics' institutes and the Society for the Diffusion of Useful Knowledge.[6] Birkbeck, a Yorkshireman educated in science and medicine in London and Edinburgh - where he and Brougham were college friends - had given pioneering lectures to working men at the Andersonian Institution in Glasgow, and had continued this interest after he left

---

[*] Birkbeck College, University of London, descends from the Mechanics' Institute.

to practise medicine in London, in 1804. His lectures were the basis of his contemporary and later reputation as the 'father' and 'leading mover of the (mechanics' institute) system'. His distinctive contribution to the character of mechanics' institutes was his insistence that they should primarily be schools of science.[7] This Birkbeckian influence is evident in the stated objectives of the Huddersfield Scientific and Mechanic Institute. As well as the financial disaster, it helps to explain its failure.

From about 1840 it was being asserted by some that the mechanics' institute movement had failed, on two counts: that the institutes did not educate the working classes; and they did not teach science. But already before 1830 the narrow view of mechanics' institutes as teachers of science to artisans was beginning to give way to the Broughamite conception of them, as general cultural centres, and by the mid-1840s this was their usual function.[8] It was in this changing climate that, in May 1841, the Huddersfield Young Men's Mental Improvement Society was founded,[9] and the new climate is the starting point of an explanation of its success. That Huddersfield was successful - and, seemingly, regarded, by the end of its first decade, as uniquely so among the 600 institutes by then in existence in England[10] - is well attested: Dr Mabel Tylecote quotes four contemporary authorities who testify to this. Huddersfield was described as one of three examples of complete success, where the 'anticipations of their founders' had been 'fully realised'. It was 'the only Mechanics' Institute which had any pretensions to meet the needs of the people', and 'the best in England'. 'We know of scarcely another Institute that can compare with it. It reaches the working man and it teaches him'.[11] It did this, not by teaching large numbers of adults eager to learn the principles of science, for such numbers did not exist in Huddersfield, but by providing elementary education to semi-literate young men and boys.[12] Even these were members of an élite of two per cent of the population nationally who attended mechanics' institutes.[13] By 1859 elementary classes far outstripped all others among member institutions of the Yorkshire Union of Mechanics' Institutes, whereas, when the Huddersfield society joined it, in 1843, ten per cent of members were attending such classes.[14] But, though Huddersfield was a pioneer in providing elementary education in evening classes, its uniqueness lay less in what it taught than in its character and organisation, which arose out of the circumstances of its foundation.

The idea of forming the society originated with five young men employed and guided by Frederic Schwann, a prosperous export merchant who had previously formed a library for use by his employees. Their intentions 'were to supply in some cases the deficiency of early instruction, and to procure for others the means of further improvement'. They met, it was later recorded, in the Temperance Hotel, Cross Church Street, in May 1841, and soon afterwards, 'with 30 or so others', began holding classes 'in the large room' of the British and Foreign Society's new school in Outcote Bank, in reading, writing, arithmetic, grammar, geography, design and French; and a library was begun 'by subscription'.[15] By the time of the first 'Annual Soirée', in February 1844, additional classes

1. Frederic Schwann

2. Nelson's Buildings Inset from the New Street junction with Cloth Hall Street. The Institute occupied rooms on the first floor of the building on New Street above the shop next to 'Smiles and Dawson', at the corner with Cloth Hall Street

had begun in elocution, vocal music, mathematics, chemistry and ornamental design. There was by then a total membership of 410, 'chiefly operatives' enjoying 'the advantages of an elementary education adapted to their occupations in life'. To the then library of 271 volumes, during 1844, 'in a spirit of liberality above all praise Mr Schwann's workmen merged their library', to make a total of 773 volumes. 'General lectures' were given, but their number was restricted, so as not to interfere with 'the more necessary branches of elementary instruction'.[16] The 'higher classes' - in French, mathematics, chemistry and ornamental design - were about to be moved to Nelson's Buildings, New Street. The first printed report already described the characteristic features of what, in August 1843, had been renamed 'Mechanics' Institution': the primacy of the classes; the importance of the Library; the relative unimportance of lectures; the Committee's concern with the social and recreational development and the moral welfare of members; the availability as teachers of experienced and well-qualified staff from the Huddersfield College and Huddersfield Collegiate proprietary schools, a factor of probably-crucial importance; even the holding of meetings in the Philosophical Hall, the largest auditorium in the town.[17]

The Institution's 'Rules' provided for the annual election, by ballot among subscribing members, of a 'Board of Directors' consisting of a President and 23 others, 'to whom the care, superintendence and control of the Institution shall be confided'. The 'List of Directors' (Committee) for 1844-5 includes three of the five 'young men in the employment of F Schwann Esq'. But the 'Rules' also provided for 'The Property of the Institution to be vested ... in ... fifteen Trustees'. Headed by Schwann, the President, the trustees were all men of substantial means and status. They included Schwann's brother-in-law and business partner, S C Kell. Thus, a group of men of substance was guaranteeing financially an educational institute, in the management of which they associated with them five young men who were employed by two of their number. The Institution's 'Rules' declared its 'object' as 'being the moral and intellectual improvement of its members ...', and that 'The Institution is and shall remain unconnected with any party in politics or sect in religion'. But, again, the oldest

3. Nelson's Buildings: rental agreement extract from the Minute Book of 1841 recording the secretary's agreement with Mr Nelson for the lease of "the unoccupied room" on the first floor of the building at the junction of New Street and Cloth Hall Street "at the reduced rent of £10"

surviving record, of early 1843, is 'a Petition laid before the members for signature against the Educational clauses of Sir James Graham's Factory Bill under consideration in the House of Commons'. It attracted 130 signatures, and was part of a successful nation-wide Nonconformist protest against the provision in the Bill for religious instruction in proposed factory schools, which would have been in accordance with the teaching of the Established Church. Two million people nationally signed such petitions. The 'British School' in Outcote Bank and the Mechanics' Institution were established by the same patrons. They were middle-class Protestant Dissenters who, politically, were Liberal-radical. At the members' Annual Meeting in January 1852, Frederic Schwann, complaining that 'it is said that no religion was taught in the Institution', insisted that it promoted 'religious and moral discipline', and, since the religion taught, being 'portions of Holy Scripture', was non-sectarian, 'could safely be supported by men of every opinion'.[18]

The first paid Secretary, Robert Neil, was appointed in 1844, but he is a shadowy figure in comparison with his successor, George Searle Phillips, also known by the *nom de plume* January Searle.[19] These men were the teacher-supervisors of the Institution, and not merely administrators, and Phillips's was, perhaps more than Schwann's, as President, the formative influence in its early development. Neil was to be described by Phillips as 'a Scotch advocate of considerable talent and learning'. Since the Committee was 'satisfied of the great importance of educating the social as well as the intellectual nature' of members, he set a pattern of regular social events: monthly meetings, which evolved as occasions for talks, readings and recitals; annual local galas, in the grounds of Fixby Hall and later Kirklees Hall;* day excursions on the new railways; and Easter and Christmas entertainments. In 1844 he arranged a 'Soirée or Tea Party' for 700 in the Philosophical Hall, and a 'Rural Gala' at 'Fixby Pastures' - three miles north of Huddersfield - to which 500 members walked in procession, with a band. There, 'their female friends were awaiting them'. There were 'refreshments on the lawn, dancing on the green … a pleasant memory…' At Easter, there had been 'concerts on 10 consecutive evenings, at the rooms in New Street', and - as Neil wrote, with seemingly-inspired prescience - 'a "Polytechnic Exhibition" on a small scale was attempted with success'.[20]

Phillips, who succeeded Neil in 1846, was the philosopher, propagandist and missionary of the Huddersfield Mechanics' Institution, and it is tempting to ask how far the fame it came to enjoy by the early 1850s was based on its undoubted achievements and how far on Phillips's celebration of them. He immediately set up a probationary class for grading entrants, which he himself conducted, as well as

---

* Fixby Hall, historic home of the Thornhill family, is now the clubhouse of Huddersfield Golf Club. Kirklees Hall – from which Kirklees Metropolitan Borough took its name, but which is in Calderdale M B – was until recently the home of the Armytage family; it is now converted into 15 "luxury homes".

teaching history and geography. He re-organised the classes to establish a regular gradation of instruction; introduced revisions of the fees system in an attempt to make the Institution 'self-supporting'; began a practice of visiting the homes of absent students; and compiled statistics of student achievements and of the institute's progress.[21] His annual reports were substantial accounts, eloquent policy statements and pedagogical disquisitions. In his time, the curriculum was extended;[22] and the institute was advertised, both nationally, in his prolific writings - which extolled, as did his annual reports, the working-class character of the institute and the sterling qualities of its students[23] - and locally, by devising a system of stitching together free tracts provided by Chambers, the Edinburgh publishers, in covers announcing the Institution's classes, and having students distribute them around the district. In 1850 a 'Preliminary Savings Bank' was introduced and run at the Institution by Charles W Sikes, of the Huddersfield Banking Company. It was a forerunner of the Post Office Savings Bank, founded as such in 1861. The last notable feature of the Phillips era was the purchase of new premises, a former warehouse, Wellington Buildings, in Queen Street, which was bought for £1,025 and converted and furnished for a further £600.[24] When Phillips resigned, in 1854, there were 518 student members paying fortnightly fees of 7d (2.9p), and 58 'presentees', who were sponsored by 'Annual Members' subscribing £1 1s 0d (105p) or more, and who themselves paid 1d per week.[25]

In his earlier years, Phillips gave many of the weekly lectures. They were delivered between 8 and 10 o'clock on Saturday evenings; and for a dozen or so élite students, 'admitted by examination', 'The Literary Class' preceded them, at 7 pm, also conducted by Phillips. In this, the students engaged in 'Literary readings, Essays and Critical

4. Wellington Buildings, Queen Street

exercises', 'and it is very seldom indeed that any member of the class is absent'. Phillips left a record of the 'method of instruction (which) has been adopted with considerable success' in his geography class. It should become a favourite text among progressive educationalists.

> 'The teacher gives out a lesson for the evening, and names the pages in the class book where it is to be found. The students then open their books, and answer simultaneously the questions which are put to them. These questions are repeated again and again, until all the facts in the lesson are supposed to be mastered, when the books are closed, and the questions repeated; all the answers being given from memory ... The students are then exercised in the Maps; and thus their previously-acquired knowledge is fixed in a more definite manner upon their minds. After the outline of the country ... has been clearly defined to them, and the rivers, towns and boundaries have been well learned, the map is abandoned for the Black Board; all the students rise from their seats; and the utmost interest is evinced in this concluding part of the instruction; for now comes the real test of the knowledge and skill of the students ... Without the help of the map, they trace the outline with the Pointer upon the Black Board, and describe ... the rivers, mountains and chief towns. ... The average attendance at this class is 46 - and ... the strictest silence and order are exacted.'[26]

Phillips ended his Huddersfield career under a cloud. In the Annual Report on the year 1851 he was listed as only 'Acting Secretary', and in those for 1852 and 1853 his name did not appear. The Committee had complained about him at the Annual Meeting in January 1852. 1853, in his words, was 'a critical year'. He described it so partly because an annual grant of £80, which - as was now discovered - had been irregularly made by the Board of Trade from 1848, was to be withdrawn. This was because the institute's drawing classes did not qualify for an award, which was only available to independent Schools of Design. The atmosphere was strained for other reasons. Frederic Schwann had resigned from the Presidency immediately after his re-election in January 1853, ostensibly on the grounds of ill-health. But relations between him and Phillips had been deteriorating since January 1851 at the latest. There were several issues in dispute, the basic one being finance: Schwann did not trust Phillips. The Directors were not unanimous when Schwann retired, but during 1853 Phillips dissipated what support he had among them and was severely censured for continuous absence and neglect of his duties at the 1854 Annual Meeting. He resigned on 28 February, with typical flamboyance and insouciance. He sent a 'telegraphic message' (from Leeds), addressed to 'Edward Eastwood' (his name was Edmund, and Phillips had worked with him for eight years), the Acting President of 1853 and now a Vice-President. It read: 'Sorry to resign my post and sorrier that I cannot come to Committee tonight. Shall have to go to London tomorrow. Shall be obliged by getting leave for five days.'[27] Significantly, his successor was to be required to sign a contract accepting a 'Schedule of Duties' and 'to enter into a recognisance of £100 to secure the Committee from any deficiency or loss of cash ...' Puzzlingly, no vote of thanks to Schwann was recorded until that contained in the report to the annual meeting of January 1856, when he was made a

5. Edmund Eastwood

life member.[28] He never broke his connection with the Institution: he had closely guided it and kept it solvent till now, and he remained an annual subscriber and a generous occasional donor till his death, in 1882. His four sons followed him as benefactors, as did his grand-daughter, Ismena Holland, in the later 1960s. Phillips's was a less happy fate. He was appointed lecturer and agent for the Yorkshire Union, but resigned after less than two years. In 1860 he went to the USA, and was a journalist in Chicago and New York. He was certified insane in 1873, and died in a New Jersey asylum in 1889.[29]

The early success of the Institution was promoted by other remarkable men: the five young men who first met to form it, who included John F Brigg and George P Beaumont, the first joint (honorary) secretaries, and Samuel Hiley, all 'Directors'; and the earliest teachers, paid and unpaid, including staff from the proprietary schools, most prominent among them George D Tomlinson, first superintendent of the Art classes and a future President, and the chemist, William Marriott, also a future President. The institute was sustained by the middle-class annual subscribers, particularly the activist Committee members among them, bearing prominent Huddersfield names like Kell, Huth, Brooke, Dodds, Lowenthal, Willans, Tolson and Wright Mellor. Then there were the students, some of whom Phillips wrote about as 'proud', 'shrewd', of 'rugged nobility and manliness', 'full of broad generosity and hard work'; 'crude, uncouth and untutored', but marked by 'their native intelligence and their willingness to learn'. Of the quality of 'digests of the last lesson' which the most advanced students in his history class of 46 were required to submit the following week, he reported: 'I have been struck, not only with the clearness of the narrative, but with the reflections of the students, and the beautiful language in which these reflections have been clothed.'[30]

6. G D Tomlinson

Notes on Chapter 1

The location of unpublished sources (except note 3), is the Univ. of Huddersfield Archives [UHA]

1. UHA: 'Rules of the Scientific and Mechanic Institute ... Established 25 April 1825', p.5.
2. 'First A[nnual] R[eport] of the Directors of Huddersfield Scientific and Mechanic Institute, as laid before the General Meeting of the Society on Monday, 19 June 1826', p.3; Second AR (1827), p.4.
3. The 'Rules' were taken from those of the Leeds Mechanics' Institute (1824). W[est] Y[orkshire] A[rchive] S[ervice], K[irklees]: 'Rules of the Huddersfield Philosophical Society' (1843). (MS).
4. Mabel Tylecote, *The Mechanics' Institutes of Lancashire and Yorkshire before 1851* (Manchester, 1957), p.5, n.2.
5. Quoted in *ibid*, p.25.
6. *Cf* J F C Harrison, *Learning and Living, 1790-1900. A Study in the History of the Adult Education Movement* (London, 1961), p.63.
7. Tylecote, *op cit*, pp.5-6, 8, 12 and n.18.
8. This 'failure' is discussed by E. Royle: 'Mechanics' Institutes and the working classes, 1840-1860' in *Historical Journal* XIV, 2 (1971), pp.305-321; the changing climate in Harrison, *op cit*, pp.62-74.
9. Not May 1840, as printed on later (eg 1863) issues of the Rules; and not 'Mutual Improvement Society', as reported by G S Phillips in *Walks Around Huddersfield* (Huddersfield, 1848), p.89, and repeated, presumably following Phillips, by J Taylor Dyson (an old student) in his *History of Huddersfield* (Huddersfield, 1926), p.269. D F E Sykes *The History of Huddersfield and its Vicinity* (Huddersfield, 1898) got it right, no doubt by following the first printed Report, of February 1844.
10. About a quarter were in Yorkshire, and there were over a dozen in the Huddersfield area, where more than 30 in all were founded. J P Hemming, 'Adult Education in Huddersfield and District, 1851-1884', MEd thesis, Manchester, 1966, ch.vi; Brian Dingle, 'History of Further Education in Huddersfield and District', Dip FE thesis, Leeds Institute of Education, 1975.
11. Tylecote, *op cit*, p.190.
12. Some students were as young as nine. *Cf* '13th Report to the Committee ...', January 1854, p.9.
13. This figure is given in Tylecote, *op cit*, p.68.
14. Figures given in Royle, *op cit*, p.309.
15. This account is derived from the MS Minute Book, 1843-8, an account in G S Phillips, *Walks Around Huddersfield* (1848), the printed ARs, the historical accounts given in the Report of January 1853, and the 'Last Report of the Work of the Institute in Northumberland Street, 1884 ...' (1885); and from Tylecote, *op cit*, ch.VI. The first mention of the meeting in the Temperance Hotel is in a 'short history' in the '12th Report ...', January 1853, p.4, which was written by Phillips.
16. 'Report of the Committee ... 13 February 1844', p.11; 'Report ...' 31 January 1845 (no pagination).
17. It belonged to the Philosophical Society, later the Theatre Royal. (Demolished 1961).
18. MS Minute Book, 1843-8; 'Rules of the Mechanics' Institution ...', (1844); MS Minute Book, 1851-4, p.14. Schwann, brought up a Lutheran, adopted the faith of his wife's family, the Kells, and became a Unitarian. He was a generous donor to the fund for the building of the Unitarian Church in Fitzwilliam Street, opened in 1855 (since 1962, the Polish (Catholic) Church). In politics, like S C Kell, Schwann was a 'Manchester School' Liberal. *Cf* obituary in *Huddersfield Examiner*, 29 April 1882.
19. Phillips is discussed in Harrison, *op cit*, pp.137-144, and in J P Hemming, 'The Mechanics' Institute Movement in the Textile Districts of Lancashire and Yorkshire in the second half of the Nineteenth Century', unpublished PhD thesis, Leeds, 1974, pp.567-8.
20. 'Report ... 31 January 1845'; eg. 'Report of the Committee ... January 1847', pp.24-5. Phillips on Neil is in '12th Report ... 29 January, 1853', p.5.
21. 'Report to the Committee ... 29 Jan. 1848', 3; '8th Report ... Jan. 1849', 6; '10th Report ... Jan. 1851', 5.
22. He fought to retain Chemistry. Latin was introduced in 1852. '13th Report ... January 1854, 10.
23. '8th Report ... January 1849', 6.
24. '10th Report ... January 1851', 5.
25. '13th A[nnual] R[eport] ... January 1854'.
26. 'Report ... 29 January 1848'.
27. MS Minute Book, 1851-4, *passim*; AR ... 27 January 1852, 10-11; AR ... 9 January 1854, 29. The name 'Batty' appears four times in Phillips's Minute Book: actually Joseph Batley.
28. '13th Report ... January 1854, 4; 15th Report ... January 1856', 7.
29. Obituary, *The Times*, 2 February 1889; *Dictionary of National Biography (DNB)*.
30. Annual Reports, *passim*. The remaining two were Charles Kay, in the 1860s and 1870s, a member of the Committee of the Yorkshire Union, and "Mr Mitchell", a migrant to the USA. ('Last Report of the Work of the Institute in Northumberland Street ... 1884', 11); 'Report ... 29 January 1848', 19-20.

CHAPTER 2

II. Architectural detail, Ramsden Building

CHAPTER 2

THE TRANSITION TO TECHNICAL SCHOOL, 1854-83

Phillips's successor, Frank Curzon, was less volatile and flamboyant, but no less vigorous in promoting the Institution's interests and reputation. Like Phillips, he became - though nine years after he left Huddersfield - 'organising agent and lecturer' to the Yorkshire Union. Unlike Phillips, he was to remain long in that post - till 1903, when he was 83 - and was to be present as its holder when the new Huddersfield Technical School was opened in 1883.[1] An artist, he built up a national reputation for his 'blackboard lectures', and was an organisation man and a statistics compiler. His energy and reforming zeal are evident in the annual reports for his time, 1854-62. A prize scheme and distribution ceremony were introduced, to encourage discipline and reward regular attendance and good conduct, as well as high standards, and a donation towards the prize fund was made by the Prince Consort.[2] Curzon successfully instituted a recruitment drive; the 'monthly meetings' became fortnightly; Saturday conferences between teachers and Directors were introduced; and a system of 'class inspections' by pairs of Directors set up. In his first annual report Curzon had diagnosed two defects in the class teaching: over-dependence on unpaid teachers, and the use of out-dated text books. The 'Directors', as Curzon preferred to call 'the Committee', were reported as aiming to increase the number of paid teachers, though still in 1861 these did not outnumber the 'voluntary' teachers. The report on the year 1855 ended with a homily on the Institution's being well supported by 'men in authority', but 'weak where it should look for strength. Its own members are the least consistent and the least grateful of its friends'. Members were educated, and rose in the world, Curzon complained, but then forgot their Institution. In the next report, and thereafter elaborated into what became a standard form, appeared tables showing the previous educational attainments of entrants, and their occupational groupings.[3] Curzon represented the Committee as being anxious to preserve the working-class nature of the Institution, as Phillips had, and in 1859 presented to a Bradford conference of social scientists a paper to demonstrate this. Yet in these years the reports strike a new tone, of middle-class respectability, and a correspondent to the *Huddersfield Chronicle* complained that 'not one-sixth of the new committee can be called working class' and that the elections to it were 'a mere farce'. But Curzon's figures substantiated his claim of the predominantly working-class composition of the student body; and this was celebrated when 'the greatest friend of popular education now living', Lord Brougham, addressed the annual soirée on 19 October 1860.[4]

As the Phillips, so the Curzon era was marked by a move to new premises, this time to the first purpose-built accommodation, in Northumberland Street. Donations for the building fund were being raised from November 1856, the leading 'influential gentlemen' in the moves being G D Tomlinson and John Brooke, whose textile firm, at Armitage Bridge, was one of the leading donors, after the principal single source of funds, the proceeds of a Ladies' Bazaar, which amounted to £1,336-2s-8d. Other main contributors were Sir John William Ramsden and Messrs Starkey Brothers, of Longroyd Bridge, whose textile workers, like those of John Brooke and Sons, are listed by the dozen among subscribers to the fund. The co-operation of the Whig grandee with the Tory factory owners - all of them Anglicans, as was Curzon - is a striking illustration of

7. Mechanics' Institution, Northumberland Street, occupied by the college between 1861 and 1883

how the Mechanics' Institution was supported across the political spectrum. In a parliamentary by-election in 1853, Joseph Starkey, JP, as Conservative candidate, had been defeated by the Liberal, Viscount Goderich*, who was Huddersfield's MP till the general election of 1857. The foundation stone of the new building was laid in October 1859 by Goderich's wife, by now Countess de Grey and Ripon, at a ceremony attended by national and local dignitaries and by 700 class pupils, and the building - on which 'not a penny has been spent on useless decoration' (but which the complainant to the *Huddersfield Chronicle* described as 'not only plain but positively ugly') - was occupied in February 1861. The Queen Street premises were sold to the Church Institute for £1,000, and the Institution was free from debt after raising a total of over £4,600 for the building and its furniture and fittings.[5]

The Institution was flourishing, and Curzon's later reports convey the optimism and confidence of these prosperous years: 'never was the need for education so widely accepted among the industrial classes' as in 1860, and there was an increase in the membership, perhaps, Curzon neatly suggested, because there were more paid teachers, for which the Institution was partly indebted to a gift of £100 over four years by Frederic Schwann.[6] 'Prosperity' enveloped the college in 1861, Curzon's last full year. The total paid-up membership was 1,216, and since 1854 the number of weekly classes in the 'evening school' had risen from 73 to 92, taught by 20 paid and 25 voluntary teachers. There were separate 'junior' (for boys 9 to 16) and 'senior' elementary classes, in which mainly the three Rs were taught, and 'special', or advanced, classes, in history, French, mathematics, drawing, book-keeping and - revived that year - chemistry. Thus, the only recognisable 'science' was chemistry, which, though it had been taught intermittently since 1844, by William Marriott - who was a manufacturing chemist as well as a teacher - did not become a sustainable subject until George Jarmain took it over, in 1864.[7] Besides the classes, and lectures - which were of three types, 'public', 'monthly' and 'class', but

---

* Whose father was Prime Minister at the time of his birth, and who was born at 10 Downing Street.

which were never given precedence - the other principal features of the Institution were the Library and the Reading Room. The Library, which benefited from gifts by Sir Robert Peel,[8] son of the late Prime Minister, had 2,000 rising to 3,000 volumes in these years; and the Reading Room, which was open, by subscription, to non-members of the Institution, was a prominent attraction in the town, for the range of newspapers it took.

But despite the prosperity, the educational base was narrow, and it is true to say that 'from educational bankruptcy the mechanics' institutes were rescued by two timely developments - the examination system of the Society of Arts and the demand for technical and scientific education'.[9] As a direct consequence of the Great Exhibition of 1851 there was created, in 1857, the Department of Science and Art, set up as part of the Education Department of the Privy Council to deal with secondary and technical education. In 1860 it instituted an examination system which - though its syllabuses were notoriously theoretical and lacking in any requirement of industrial experience - was to last for 40 years. The Science and Art Department gave approval for the setting up of 'science schools', many of them in mechanics' institutes, to which it gave grants, on a 'payment by results' (in examinations) basis. The Society of Arts began its examining in 1856, and in 1857 held an experimental 'Prize Examination', 'to include Commercial and Trade Schools', choosing the Huddersfield Institution as its only centre outside London.[10] Frank Curzon had warned his students of their disadvantage in competing in this examination with people 'from middle class literary societies and private schools', but of the 90 successful candidates (from 122 entrants) 32 were from Huddersfield, and he now enthused about the 'beneficial results', showing 'the importance of accuracy ... and ... of clear expression', and about how people who had known nothing of the Institution 'now realise its value'.[11] In 1873 the Society of Arts was to enter the field of technical education, but it handed these subjects over to the newly-established City & Guilds of London Institute (CGLI) in 1880.[12] The first Huddersfield science students to be examined were members of George Jarmain's organic and inorganic chemistry classes, who took the Science and Art Department's examinations in 1865. From 1867 candidates were entered from the elementary classes for the examinations of the Yorkshire Union Board of Education, and the best of them were also candidates for the Society of Arts examinations; and from 1869 students in the drawing classes were examined by the Science and Art Department. By then, too, students in other subjects than chemistry took the science examinations, the range of 'Science Classes' having been extended to include Plane and Solid Geometry, Mechanical and Machine Drawing, Magnetism and Electricity, and Acoustics, Light and Heat.[13]

8. Frank Curzon, Secretary, Mechanics' Institution, 1854-62

The term 'technical education' was first used in an annual report in 1867, when the

9. George Jarmain: teacher of Chemistry

Secretary, Joseph Bate, expounding on 'this important subject', claimed that the Committee had fostered it 'from almost the commencement of the institution'. Nationally and locally, an important part of the impetus towards its promotion came from the shock to British complacency given by the Paris Exhibition of 1867. An outcome of this was the setting up of a Parliamentary Committee on Scientific Instruction. One witness called before it told the Committee: 'I do not know of a single manager of an ironworks in Yorkshire who understands the elements of chemistry'. The Committee's report would show that there were 60 science schools, with 2,520 pupils, in Lancashire, but only 16 schools, with 476 pupils, in Yorkshire.[14] In Huddersfield, the Annual Report on the year 1868 spoke of 'reports of practical men who visited the Paris Exhibition' warning that 'the technical education which the operatives on the continent possess may imperil our industrial prosperity'. It boasted about 'the practical direction of the teaching of the Institution', and especially about two developments of that year: the introduction of a class in the chemistry of dyeing, taught by Mr Jarmain, who was one of the 'practical men who visited the Paris Exhibition'; and, in conjunction with the Yorkshire Board of Education, the establishment of 'Science Classes for schoolmasters and others in practical geometry and machine drawing'. This latter was the first form of teacher training at Huddersfield Mechanics' Institution.[15]

The implementation of the Elementary Education Act of 1870 in Huddersfield was eventually to help to change the character and identity of the Mechanics' Institution, because it would take away a large part of its traditional work, and cause it to seek new functions. An immediate consequence, however, was that its implementation added to the Institution's sources of income: as well as members' subscriptions and grants from the Science and Art Department based on examination successes, it now also received annual allowances for its elementary classes from the Education Department of the Privy Council; and after 1873 annual examinations of students in the (elementary) 'Evening Classes' were conducted by HM Inspectors of Schools (HMI). At the time of the Institution's annual meeting of January 1876, the *Huddersfield Chronicle* commented that, nearly five years after the formation, under the Act, of the Huddersfield School Board, there were in the town both 'elementary schools in super-abundance and a Mechanics' Institute preparing to enlarge its classrooms. These two facts ... seem to bear the relations of cause and effect'. The Institution it described as 'a great society, quite as worthy as it is able to undertake the higher duties that lie before it'.[16] The annual report of 1879 expressed surprise that 'despite such opportunities to the masses to gain Elementary Education' (as the Board Schools provided), the attendance at the Institution's elementary classes did not fall more.[17] Only in January 1883 did the new Secretary, Austin Keen, remark on 'the decline of the elementary classes', explaining it as 'naturally consequent upon the Compulsory Education Act of 1876'.

This report shows the extent of the changes in the Institution since 1870. It divided it into the 'Technical School', which taught Cloth Manufacture, and had a small, newly-formed Mechanical Engineering class, both subjects examined by the CGLI; the 'Science School' and the 'School of Art', whose students were examined by the Science and Art Department; 'Higher Grade' classes in French, German, English Literature and commercial subjects, examined, if and as appropriate, by the Society of Arts or the Yorkshire Union's Board of Education; and the elementary classes, inspected by HMI. Keen's report quoted from the 'Education Blue Book', a government publication of August 1882, which was written by A P Graves, HMI*, on evening schools nationally: 'The one notable exception to this want of success is that of "the Huddersfield Mechanics" Institute Night School', which numbers some 300 male pupils and is worked by a large and efficient staff of teachers under a most active and intelligent committee'. A recent drive to attract middle-class participation in classes - and with it financial support - had done little to alter the social composition of the Institution. In a total membership of 1,500, from the list of 900 'Ordinary and Presentee Members' (the latter paying 3½d per week for classes), 395 were 'Factory Operatives' and 159 'Clerks and Office Boys'. Only 40 members were listed as 'Mechanics', fewer than the 42 'Pupil Teachers'.[18] Such was the composition and such the reputation of the Institution to which, 'just before Whit', 1883, the Committee of the Huddersfield Female Educational Institute - which had been formed in 1846 under the same auspices as the Mechanics' Institution - 'formally handed over "their work" ' and left their Beaumont Street premises to join the hitherto-all-male Institution (except for singing classes) in its new building in Queen Street South. In its first year two female classes were to be formed, with, disappointingly, only twelve members each.[19]

The Institution's move to a new building and its transformation into the 'Technical and Trade School' were the result of nearly ten years' planning and negotiation. The need for more accommodation, to house the expanding science and technical classes, was pressing from the mid-1870s, when the *Huddersfield Chronicle* foresaw for the Institution a role as a 'Mechanics' college' undertaking 'the higher duties that lie before it'.[16] In April 1877, a meeting took place between deputations from the Committee of the Mechanics' Institution and the Council of the Chamber of Commerce, which two months earlier had resolved that the trustees of several local charities be invited to confer with the Chamber about the possible transfer of the funds from the charities to a proposed 'Trade School', 'working for the benefit of local industry and commerce'.[20] The Institution's deputation was led by John Fligg Brigg, JP, the President, who had been one of Mr Schwann's young employees who met in the temperance hotel in 1841, and who was

10. Alderman John Fligg Brigg

---

* Father of Robert Graves, and author of many volumes of Irish songs and ballads. He composed the popular song, 'Father O'Flynn'.

now himself a prosperous merchant and a leading citizen. Its other members were also long-term supporters and Directors: Edward Huth, JP, and Councillor William Marriott, the chemist; and the Secretary, Joseph Bate. The Council of the Chamber of Commerce contained six men who were or had been Committee members of the Institution, two of whom were ex-Presidents. A report of the meeting was published, addressed to 'subscribers and the public generally', describing a proposal by the joint committee for a Trade School, which the Council would 'consider'.[21] What seemed a potential threat to the future of the Mechanics' Institution was averted by the adoption in November, by the joint committee of the Chamber and the Institution, of a scheme for a Technical School, the name of which would be 'Huddersfield Technical School and Mechanics' Institution'.

A year later the Charity Commissioners authorised the trustees of the Armitage Charity to use the charity's income to support the proposed school; the trustees of the Nettleton and Wormald charities were later also given authority to make annual grants. By the end of 1879 it had been agreed that a plan for an extension of the Mechanics' Institution to house the new Technical School should be prepared by the architect, Edward Hughes, at an estimated cost of £11,000, to provide both 'scientific instruction for youths on leaving school' and 'day classes for the sons of manufacturers'. A report of the joint committee's work, signed by its chairman, Thomas Brooke, head of the firm of John Brooke & Sons, who was now President of both the Chamber of Commerce and the Mechanics' Institution, and the driving force behind the scheme, was issued in December and called on the public to support the venture.[22] But in June 1880 it was accepted that a new site would have to be found, to allow future expansion, and by March 1881 Edward Hughes's plans for a new building on Queen Street South, on a site leased from the Ramsden Estate Trustees for 999 years, had been adopted. A building fund was created, which reached over £15,500,

11. Huddersfield Technical School in the 1880s

12. Sir John William Ramsden

including a £2,000 donation from the Worshipful Company of Clothworkers of the City of London. Since 1878 the Company had been contributing £100 per annum 'to the Technical School of the Institution'. It had also established two scholarships, to be competed for annually by members of the Designing and Weaving classes, tenable at the Yorkshire College, Leeds. This was the forerunner of the University of Leeds, and the Clothworkers' Company had been its main financial support since its foundation in 1874.[23] The Master of the Company, the Rev Alfred Child, laid the memorial stone of the new building on 21 October 1881,[24] and the project - the front half of the total plan, and of the present building - was completed in May 1883. In contrast with the Northumberland Street building, money was spent on 'decoration' of this new building: on the facade were set four lions rampant, holding shields, displaying the arms of the 'Worshipful Guild of Clothworkers', the Borough of Huddersfield, Sir John Ramsden, Bart, MP, and Thomas Brooke, later Sir Thomas Brooke, Bart. The first function held in the building was a Fine Art and Industrial Exhibition, which was opened at the same time as the building itself, by the Duke of Somerset, father-in-law of Sir John Ramsden, on 7 July 1883, and which, before it closed, on 29 December, was visited by 329,629 people. Present at the opening ceremony, as ex-Mayor of Huddersfield and as a Vice-President of the Institution - and who had been, and was to be again, its President - was Alderman John Fligg Brigg, JP.[25] The first academic function in the building was a prize distribution, held on 18 December, 1883, at which the Secretary and Director of the City and Guilds of London Institute, Philip Magnus, gave the prizes. So extensive was the exhibition that the building was not cleared for teaching until Michaelmas (29 September) 1884.

Notes on Chapter 2

The location of unpublished sources cited in these notes, and in the notes of subsequent chapters, is the University of Huddersfield Archives [UHA]

1. *Cf* F Curzon, *Reminiscences of My Life Work* (Leeds, 1904), which is not most notable for its modesty.
2. '16th Report ... January 1857', p.8; '18th Report ... January 1859', p.9.
3. '14th Report ... January 1855', p.13; '15th Report ... January 1856', pp.14-15.
4. *Huddersfield Chronicle*, 2 February 1861; 20th Annual Report (AR) ... January 1861, p.6. Over the years 1859 to 1882, the percentage of 'factory operatives' in the Huddersfield student body was 32; 'mechanics', so called, constituted 5.5 per cent. The most expanded category over the period was that of 'clerks and bookkeepers'.
5. 21st AR ... January 1862, 4; 'List of Subscribers for the Erection of the New Building ... 1861'. Other generous donors were T P Crosland, JP - Huddersfield's first Conservative MP, 1865-8 - 'who placed the site for the building at our command, and ... Mr J W Carlile, who divided with us the responsibility for its purchase'. (MS Minute Book, 1858-9, 33.) The building, empty since it was abandoned by the Friendly and Trades Club in the early 1980s, has recently been renovated and converted. The Queen Street building is the only one occupied by the Mechanics' Institution that is not still standing.
6. 19th AR ... January 1860, p.3; 20th AR ... January 1861, p.4.
7. 15th AR ... January 1855; 21st AR ... January 1862, p.8.
8. 16th Report ... January 1857, p.4.
9. J F C Harrison, *op cit*, p.213.
10. Society of Arts Examination Notice, June 1857.
11. 16th and 17th Reports ... January 1857, 1858, pp.12, 3-4.
12. Michael Argles, *South Kensington to Robbins. An Account of English Technical and Scientific Education since 1851* (London, 1964), pp.16-25.
13. ARs for years 1865-9.
14. 'Select Committee on Scientific Instruction', Parliamentary Papers (PP), 1867-68, XV. Quoted in Argles, *op cit*, p.26.
15. 28th AR ... January 1869. Jarmain's letter to the *Huddersfield Examiner*, 4th January 1868, advocating the establishment of a 'Central School of Industry' in 'some central town of the West Riding, say Leeds', cannot have pleased the Institution's Directors.
16. 35th AR ... January 1876; *Huddersfield Chronicle*, 5 February 1876.
17. 39th AR ... January 1880, p.7.
18. AR ...1882; AR... January 1883.
19. AR ... January 1884, p.21.
20. *Huddersfield Examiner*, 24 February 1877.
21. The two ex-Presidents were John Dodds and Wright Mellor. 'Trade School for Huddersfield. Report of an interview ... on Wednesday, 11th April, 1877'.
22. 'Scheme for a Technical School for Huddersfield and Report of the Committee on the Huddersfield Technical School and Mechanics' Institute', December 1879.
23. AR for 1884 (1885), pp.16-17; P H J H Gosden and A J Taylor, *History of the University of Leeds, Studies in the History of a University, 1874-1974* (Leeds, 1975), pp.84-6.
24. 38th AR ... January 1879, p.8; 41st AR ... January 1882, p.19.
25. AR ... 1883 (1884), p.25; *Huddersfield Examiner,* 7 July 1883 and Supplement, p.2; *Huddersfield Chronicle*, 14 July 1883.

CHAPTER 3

III. St. Paul's.

CHAPTER 3

THE FIRST AGE OF TECHNICAL EDUCATION, 1884-1914

(a) The Road to Municipalisation, 1884-1903

The Mechanics' Institution had formally been preserved, but effectively had been absorbed into the new 'Technical School'. The 'Committee of Directors' was replaced by 'Governors', constituted as a public educational trust. There were five '*Ex Officio*' governors - representing public bodies, and one of whom was the Mayor of Huddersfield - and five 'Nominated' governors - representing the contributing charities - as well as the 18 'Representative' governors still elected at annual meetings of members. The transformation was made the more necessary because the development by the Huddersfield School Board of 'evening continuation schools' from the late 1880s and its opening of a Higher Grade School in 1894 were to take over both the post-school elementary education needed in the town and some of the post-elementary scientific or technical teaching.[1] Another formative influence on the character of the institution was a powerfully-expressed body of opinion that it should not be merely a technical institute. The Conservative *Huddersfield Chronicle* had supported the idea of a technical school, but had pleaded for a traditional liberal education to be preserved. When the Marquess of Ripon, the former MP for Huddersfield, and Viceroy of India from 1880 to 1884 - who had supported the institute from its early days, and whose wife had, in 1859, laid the foundation stone of the Northumberland Street building - formally inaugurated classes in the new building, in a ceremony in the new Town Hall, in March 1885, he hoped that 'literature, history, geography, economics, music and the classics' would be taught. The Liberal *Huddersfield Examiner*, reporting this, supported his plea, on the grounds that much of the fund subscribed, especially from the charities, was earmarked for the support of general education. The President, Thomas Brooke, expressed the same hope at a ceremony for the dedication of memorial windows in the new building on 14 July 1885.[2] There had also been deliberate attempts to widen the social basis of the student body: in 1879 an evening class had been put on in Weaving and Designing 'for the sons of manufacturers, merchants and others', and in 1881 this became a day class, out of reach of apprentices; likewise in 1879, an afternoon French class 'for ladies' had been established, and in 1880 a 'Select Morning class for Ladies in Art'.[3]

The Technical School and Mechanics' Institute of 1884 was organised academically into a Technical School, a Science School and a School of Art; it also offered 'advanced' classes in modern languages and commerce, and for London University matriculation and the preliminary examinations of professional bodies in law and accountancy; and it advertised a class for pupil teachers in Board Schools. It still provided elementary classes every night of the week, separately for 'boys and girls', 'young men and women' and 'persons of 21 years and upwards'. Twenty years later, the academic range of what by then had become a municipal technical college would again come under scrutiny, in circumstances radically changed by the interaction of national and local pressures, and the college would again preserve its broadly-based curriculum.

In that interval technical education nationally advanced more rapidly than at any time previously. Already in 1883-4, a Royal Commission on Technical Instruction had produced five volumes of recommendations. Some members of the commission were founders of the National Association for the Promotion of Technical and Secondary Education, which in 1889 published *Technical Education in England and Wales*, a critical survey of the provision of technical education, with recommendations for its improvement. In particular, it called for a system of secondary schools, and for co-ordination of the work of central and local educational agencies. In the same year the Technical Instruction Act enabled the new County and County Borough Councils set up by the Local Government Act of 1888 to establish secondary and technical schools, and finance them from the rates; and in 1890 the Local Taxation (Customs and Excise) Act allowed these local authorities to subsidise technical education out of the revenue from certain customs and excise duties (what came to be known as 'whisky money'). Thus, there were henceforth two authorities locally providing or financing education: the School Boards set up under the 1870 Act to provide elementary education, but by the 1890s using the government's new 'Education Codes' to provide 'evening continuation schools' and 'higher-grade schools'; and the County and County Borough Councils, supporting technical education through their Technical Instruction Committees. This over-lapping of authority was removed through the 'Cockerton judgments' of 1900 and 1901, which determined that expenditure by School Boards on evening-continuation and higher-grade schools was illegal. Accordingly, the 1902 Education Act abolished the *ad hoc* School Boards and made the Councils the Local Education Authorities (LEA), empowered to develop 'elementary and other than elementary education', which meant secondary, technical and adult education, and teacher training. Already, in 1899, the Board of Education had been established, absorbing the old Education Department of the Privy Council and the Schools section of the Charity Commission.[4]

Within the newly-constituted College, 'the signs of the times', and proof, it was claimed, that 'our school is established on a sound basis', were 'the steady decline of the elementary classes and the contemporaneous rise of the higher ones'.[5] The first Principal, Dr G S Turpin, was appointed in 1894. But he left at the end of 1895 and was succeeded by Dr S G Rawson, like Dr Turpin, a chemist. At the same time, the institution officially changed its name and status, and became 'The Huddersfield Technical College', comprising a Technical School, a Science School, a School of Art, and a Mechanics' Institute, hereinafter called 'The College'.[6] The old Mechanics' Institution building in Northumberland Street had been sold in 1887 for £525, and a fund was opened for a 'Jubilee Extension' (completion) of the new building. This fund, to which Sir Joseph Crosland - Conservative MP for Huddersfield, 1893-5, and proprietor of the

13. The Marquess of Ripon

Huddersfield Chronicle - donated £5,500, was allowed to accumulate for ten years. Building was begun in 1897 and completed in 1900 at a cost of over £32,000. The College then had 1,335 students, an increase of 20 per cent over the number in 1894. The extension almost doubled the size of the building, and provided new laboratories and art studios, a gymnasium and a museum. But even after this expenditure, the Principal considered the equipment available was 'not yet fully capable of meeting the demands which may be made by the inhabitants of Huddersfield'.[7]

14. Sir Joseph Crosland

This remark was made in the knowledge that the College was to be transferred to the control of Huddersfield Corporation, a move dictated by financial necessity. In the next year's *Calendar*, that for 1902-3, which was the last under the old régime, the Secretary, Thomas Thorp, recorded that the Huddersfield Corporation Bill had received Royal Assent in July 1902. He then gave an historical survey since 1841, and indulged in some self-congratulatory thoughts on the 'excellent provision now made for the teaching of Science, Art, Technological, Literary, Commercial and other subjects'. Though education facilities had multiplied in Huddersfield since 1884, the College, he reported, 'continued its successful career'.[8] But the transfer, which took effect on 1 April 1903, was necessary for its survival. It had been in financial difficulties from, at the latest, 1888, when the Governors were looking to 'find new ways of bringing the income up to the expenditure'. In March 1890 they sent a deputation to the new County Borough Council to ask for an annual contribution of £600. This would have represented a rate of less than a halfpenny in the pound, and the Technical Instruction Act empowered the Council to levy a penny rate to support technical education.[9] But the Council refused to levy any rate, and the only money the College received from the Council - as also from the West Riding County Council - was 'whisky money', which was passed on from 1891, and which, over the next twelve years, amounted to £14,240. Although the first report acknowledging receipt of this money also speaks of the 'need of an increased assured annual income', reports after that for the year 1899-90 are obsequious in their gratitude to the Corporation for its 'handsome contributions', describing them as an 'important factor in the development of the college'.[10] Negotiations for the transfer of the College to Council control began in June 1899. As the bills for the new extensions came in, it was clear that the burden of 'working and maintaining the college has become almost too great to be borne by a private body'.[11] When the building and equipment, including the library of 9,000 volumes, were made over, under the Huddersfield Corporation Act, the College's debt on current account was not less than £9,000, and on the building account £23,500. The college therefore began its municipal career with a capital debt of over £32,000.[12]*
The 1902 Education Act, a measure of Balfour's Conservative Government, was not well

---

* This was the debt taken over by Huddersfield Corporation. Its rough equivalent today is £1.6m.

15. Technical School, Huddersfield

received in Liberal-dominated Huddersfield. But in so far as it removed the School Board, it removed a thorn from the side of the Technical College: since 1894 the Board's Higher Grade School had taken pupils from the College's 'Day Science School', and its pupil-teacher centres had undermined the College's centre.[13]

Dr Rawson began the practice of presenting annual reports, which, in his time, were additional to the Secretary's. He made them vehicles for publicising his thoughts on the state of education generally, his ambitions for the College, and his hopes and frustrations. His over-riding concern was to raise the academic standards and the status of the College. There emerges from the addresses he gave at December prize-givings between 1896 and 1902 an ideal of a college where higher-level work is done, over a range of subjects including the Arts as well as Science and Technology, and 'Higher Commercial Studies'. Students would develop a collegiate spirit, fostered through student societies. The success of the College's 'Central Classes for Pupil Teachers' made the case, he argued, for the establishment of a Day Training College for Teachers within it. In 1902, three students graduated with honours BSc degrees of London University, one of them, George Kaye - a future FRS - with First Class honours, and there were now also BA honours students. Dr Rawson received coldly an invitation from the Court of the Victoria University for the College to be affiliated, thereby sending its students for their final two years to one of the University's constituent colleges, at Manchester, Liverpool or Leeds. He discouraged his students' pursuit of university scholarships: Huddersfield 'could train students as well as elsewhere'. His ambition was thus for Huddersfield to become a University College. To that end, he successfully campaigned for appointments to lectureships in Economics and in Latin and Greek, 'for no education ... can be efficient and lasting unless based upon a thoroughly sound liberal education of the conservative type'. The strengthening of the staff 'on the literary side' Dr Rawson viewed 'with special pleasure', for there was 'need ... for advanced work of other types than that which is usually associated with the word technical ...'. Hence, too, his strengthening of 'the academic content' of the Library, and promotion of the Museum (used especially in teaching biology), which provided, he thought, the 'concrete', as the Library provided the 'abstract' support to higher-level studies.

Conditions in all 'Technical Institutions', he complained, were 'extremely unsatisfactory', because they were 'in situations where attendance is not compulsory'. They had the buildings, the staff and the equipment, 'but no effort is made to see that students in due balance are provided'. Instead, both employers and parents wanted students 'to sever all connection at the earliest possible moment'. Attendance at night school was 'accepted as both right and fitting', and only the tired students made a sacrifice. The comparisons Dr Rawson made with conditions in German Technical High Schools are a valuable contemporary record and make a telling criticism of English provision for higher technical education. For Huddersfield, immediately, he hoped that the new LEA would co-ordinate the education service; that at least the Evening Continuation Schools and the Technical College would be linked; and that the work done in schools might bear some regulated relationship to what at least some former pupils would do at the College. He advocated that an entrance examination be introduced for day students, and a minimum-age limit imposed; that the new Education Committee make regulations to provide a flow of the more-able students in its schools to the College, and 'that they should attend day classes, on at least two or three half days a week'. 'The junior and weaker portion' of school leavers should be excluded from the College, and if the 'Day School of Science', with its under-16 pupils, were removed, room could be found to house the needed Day Teacher Training College.[14]

16. Professor Michael Sadler

(b) The Pre-War Municipal Technical College, 1903-14

The County Borough of Huddersfield inherited a College of 1,335 students, 377 of them women. An army of HM Inspectors had recently declared it to be in a very healthy state. After 'numerous visits' they had praised it for its 'comprehensive curriculum', and found 'the work of the College ... very satisfactory'. There had been 'much progress ... in the development of the day technical departments ...'; 'the staff (was) an exceptionally strong one'; 'and the organisation of teaching (left) little to be desired'.[15] Charged with implementing the 1902 Act, like eight other of the new LEAs, Huddersfield invited a nationally-acknowledged expert, Michael Sadler, formerly senior official in the Education Department, and now part-time Professor of Educational Administration at Manchester University, to make recommendations on the provision of secondary and technical education in the borough.[16]

Sadler found advising on the College the most difficult part of his commission. He praised 'the pioneers of technical education in Huddersfield' who had 'started' 'the Technical College in 1884 on so ambitious a scale', but felt that it had suffered from the

17. Ramsden Building with its 1900s extension.

absence of a good public secondary school in the town in the last 20 years, and from the fact that 'the West Riding believes in the practical man' and 'distrusts the theorist'. Having surveyed its 13 departments, he concluded that the College should concentrate its efforts on those in which the work 'stood in vital relations to the industries of the Borough: the Textile, Art, Dyeing (and closely associated Chemical Department) and Mechanical and Electrical Engineering Departments'. The College had not impressed itself 'on the mind of Huddersfield as an essential factor in its future industrial prosperity', and to change public sentiment it would be necessary to make the College 'plainly and unmistakably an institution devoted to the interests of the staple trade of the town'. Any thought of making it 'a University College with a wide range of academic activities' must be banished. 'The University of Leeds is within easy reach, and can meet all ordinary needs ... The right policy for Huddersfield is to strengthen the University of Leeds* ...', and, like Bradford, to concentrate on developing 'at home' those technical departments which could 'help the trade and add to the wealth of the community'. For this to happen there had to be a first-rate public boys' secondary school to guarantee the success of the College's day classes, and good elementary and evening schools to provide pupils for its evening classes. The 'Day School of Science', which had competed unfavourably with the town's Higher Grade School, should be abolished, and when it was, the College's Department of Languages - teaching Latin and Greek, English, French and German - would not have enough advanced students preparing for the London external BA degree to justify its existence. The Department of Commerce taught 'elementary commercial work', which was 'utterly out of place in the technical college', and the work of the Department of Economics should go to the University of Leeds. The

---

* The University of Leeds had been created that year, 1904, separated from The Victoria University. The Victoria University of Manchester and the University of Liverpool, the other former constituents of The Victoria University (created in 1874), had received their charters in 1903. Firth College, Sheffield, became a university in 1905. The other English universities then were Oxford, Cambridge, London (1834), Durham (1836) and Birmingham (1900). There were University Colleges at Southampton, Newcastle, Bristol, Nottingham, Reading and Exeter, whose students were awarded their degrees by the University of London, or, in the case of Newcastle, by the University of Durham.

18. Museum Room, Huddersfield Technical School

College had 'one of the best biological departments in the North of England'. Its students included elementary teachers preparing for their certificates, a few students working for London BSc degrees, and pharmaceutical students. Under its head, Mr Woodhead, the Department did useful research work, and its best future, Sadler said, would be affiliation with the University. The Mathematics Department would, as at Bradford, be best incorporated into the Engineering departments; and the Department of Domestic Economy should be merged with one of the LEA's Evening Continuation centres. The chief question regarding the Education Department - from 1904 the only pupil-teacher centre in the town[17] - was whether it would be wise to establish a Day Training College. Sadler came down against this, in the interests of concentrating the College's resources on its technical work.[18] Thus, on the desirability of there being well-supported day classes and on the need for co-ordination of evening-school provision in the town - though Sadler did not concede that the Technical College should do the co-ordinating - Dr Rawson and Professor Sadler agreed. On the future academic range of the College they did not, the London chemist pleading the need for a wide subject range and the Oxford classicist advocating concentration on the narrowly technical.

Perhaps through inertia - or perhaps through masterly inactivity rather than deliberate acts of policy, for there is no record of decisions - it was more the Rawson than the Sadler view of the subject coverage that prevailed. In the perspective of 100 years of English technical-further-higher education, the most significant issue dividing Rawson and Sadler was not a liberal-*versus*-technical curriculum issue, but a comprehensive-*versus*-élitist concept of higher education. There is a line of continuity between the debate in Huddersfield in 1904 and the Higher Education Act of 1991, which decreed that polytechnics and other colleges could become universities. Sadler wanted to restrict the number of university-type institutions to what could be sustained by the number of students qualified. Rawson was frustrated because he knew many more were capable of being qualified. The disputants never met. Professor Sadler did his fieldwork in Huddersfield in the early months of 1904 - that at the College he did in March - and Dr Rawson had left in early January, to become Worcestershire's first Director of Education. His successor did not take up his post till September. It would have been awkward if Rawson had remained Principal, since the Sadler report dismissed so brusquely the academic ambitions he had held, and publicly advocated, for the College.

Immediate responses to the Sadler report were the closures of the College's Secondary Day and Evening Continuation Schools. The new Principal, J F Hudson, an Oxford mathematician and physicist, who came immediately from Southampton University College, continued the urgings of Dr Rawson for the establishment of a Municipal Teacher Training College,[19] but again vainly. Equally fruitless was revived talk of university-college status. In February 1905 a Treasury report had included Huddersfield among examples of colleges that might be given financial assistance to develop into university colleges, but by July this was discounted, and the College became affiliated to Leeds University for Arts and Science subjects, Engineering, Medicine, Commerce and Law. The effect of this was that students from Huddersfield day-time courses could receive one year's remission on the University's courses.[20] Already before the Sadler report had been published, Mr Hudson's first annual report had anticipated its suggestions for the College to become a 'Technical Institution' under the Board of Education's Regulations - which required it to give 'organised courses' of advanced day-time instruction - and for the status and level of work of the Textile Department to be raised; and, like Sadler, Hudson had seen the need for improved secondary-school provision in

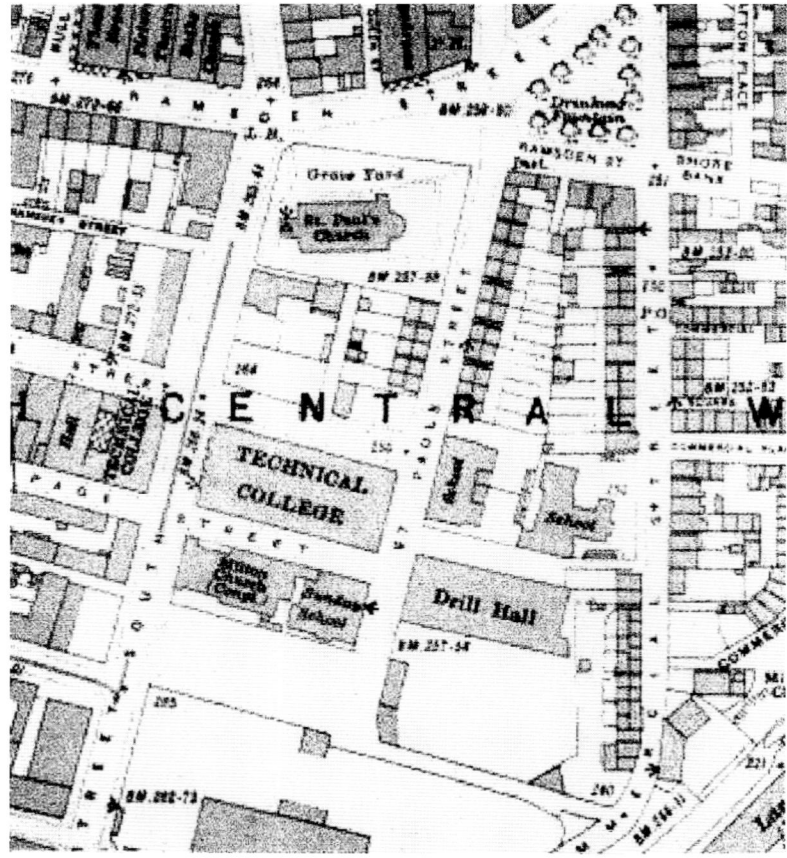
19. Ordnance Survey Map of Technical College and its surrounds

Huddersfield.[21] To raise standards and improve the supply of students to the College, the age of admission, he said, should be raised, ideally to 16; and the school-leaving age from 13 to 14 or even 15. A system of College Certificates and Diplomas was introduced for full-time students on 3-year courses and part-time students on 5-year courses, for which the first awards were made in 1908. There was an attempt to link the LEA's evening schools to the College by a system of scholarships, and 'fixed' or 'group' courses of study were arranged, to give evening students a coherent education, as Dr Rawson had advocated. Another development in the immediate post-Sadler years was co-operation in non-vocational adult evening classes with the recently-founded Workers' Educational Association (WEA), and with the longer-established Oxford Extension Movement.[22]

20. Huddersfield Technical School

Some practical Sadler - and Rawson - recommendations the LEA had ignored, and in August 1909 it received a sharply-worded report from the Board of Education on its 'Technical and Evening Schools'. The HMI authors hoped the Authority would 'see its way' to deal immediately with, *inter alia*, the retention of elementary evening-class work at the Technical College and the inadequate co-ordination of its Evening Schools with the College. Both Rawson and Sadler had called for such co-ordination, Rawson for it to be done by the College. The Board's report complained that technical education in Huddersfield was still under the management of two separate bodies - the Technical College Governors and the Higher Education Sub-committee of the Council's Education Committee - that it was administered by two separate sets of officials, and that the College Principal had no role in relation to the Evening Schools. Sadler had recommended that the Technical College Committee (Governors) and the Education Committee of the Council should be amalgamated. The Board's report still only 'suggested' that the College Governors, then being re-constituted, should have members 'more directly in touch with other branches of the educational work of the Borough'; and the Governors' existence as a Committee of Council, co-existent with, and not subordinate to, the Education Committee, went on till 1921. This 1909 report commended the 'valuable work' done in the College, and particularly the research work of some of the staff; its criticisms and suggestions were on organisational matters. It suggested that the Authority's Evening Schools should be under the Governors' control; that the Principal and a local Inspector should draw up a comprehensive scheme for these schools and have power to implement it; that the age and standard of admission to the College, which 'are very low for an institution of this character', be raised (from age 14 and 'Standard VI' of the Elementary Code); that elementary work in commercial subjects should be relegated to Evening Schools (as Sadler had recommended); that students under 19 should take a 'complete course' (as Rawson); and that the Textile Department should be extended as soon as possible.[23]

There followed a flurry of activity. Within a month a public meeting was convened in the Town Hall, at which Board of Education officials were present, on the importance of improved attendance at evening schools and the Technical College; and 2,000 workers were appealed to at dinner-hour meetings in local mills.[24] The composition of the College's governing body was changed so that it was now wholly determined by the Council's Education Committee, though it was still a separate committee of the Council.[25] The recruitment drive raised the student total slightly in 1910-11, but it fell back again, and in the last pre-war year was 1,690, some 287 of them being day students. Not rising numbers, but the rising level of work in the College caused income from government grants to rise, from £3,000 in 1908-9 to over £4,000 in 1912-13, when total annual income was £12,878.[26] There is no evidence that the Principal acted as overall co-ordinator of the town's evening schools, but closer relations with them were cultivated, and more students were admitted directly from them; and in 1911 it was considered time to raise the admission age of the College to 16, 'except for those who have completed an evening school course or are qualified by attending Secondary or Higher Elementary School', exceptions which must have largely undermined the rule.

On the eve of war the College had 42 full-time academic staff and 37 part-time teachers, and was teaching students ranging in standard from final honours of London University in Arts and Sciences (principally Chemistry), through its own Diploma and Certificate courses and courses for the examinations of public bodies and professional institutes, non-examined classes in languages, literature and history - with classes in New Testament Greek under consideration - to evening classes in grocery and the first day-release classes for apprentices. As well as its affiliated status with Leeds University, it enjoyed 'special relations' with Edinburgh University and Imperial College, London, and was an established centre for WEA and Oxford Extension lectures. Its public reading room attracted a numerous membership from the general public; it had a library of over 9,000 volumes, and a museum that provided a service to local schools, whose teachers it helped to train; and it boasted an impressive number of scholarship endowments. Its students' societies, including a Women Students' association, were flourishing; and it had just endured another inspection by 18 of HM Inspectors, whose report praised its work and stressed the need for more space, especially for its Textile Department.[27]

21. Principal J F Hudson

Notes on Chapter 3

1. *Cf* Brian D Moriarty, 'Politics and Education in Huddersfield in the late-nineteenth century', unpublished MEd thesis, Leeds, 1978, esp Chapter 8.
2. *Huddersfield Chronicle*, 7 February, 1880; *Huddersfield Examiner*, 14 March, 1885; *Huddersfield Chronicle*, 14 July, 1885.
3. AR for 1879, 1880, 1881.
4. Argles, *op cit*, chapter 3; R C K Ensor, *England 1870-1914* (Oxford, 1946), pp.305-6, pp.317-20; Michael Sanderson, *Educational Opportunity and Social Change in England* (London, 1987), pp.18-25.
5. *Calendar for 1885-6*, pp.62-3.
6. *Calendar for 1896-7*, pp.207, 215. Dr Turpin left to become Headmaster of Swansea Intermediate and Technical Schools, and was to be Headmaster of Nottingham High School, 1901-25. His grandson, the late David Newbold, was to become one of the first Professors of Huddersfield Polytechnic, in 1984.
7. *Calendars* for 1890-91, p.132; 1898, p.133; 1900-01, p.237; 1901-02, p.215. The 'Jubilee Extension' fund was raised to commemorate the Golden Jubilee of Queen Victoria's accession, 1887. Sir Joseph Crosland was the younger brother of T P who had 'facilitated' the purchase of the site of the Northumberland Street building.
8. *Calendar for 1902-03*, p.236.
9. *Calendars* for 1888-9, pp.98-9; 1890-91, p.101.
10. *Calendars* for 1892-3, pp.120, 110; 1900-01, p.203; 1902-03, p.265.
11. *Calendar* for 1900-01, p.211.
12. 'Report on Secondary and Technical Education in Huddersfield' by Michael E Sadler, 1904, p.70 (Sadler Report). Figures given in the College's annual reports do not tally with those quoted in the Sadler Report, which presumably were provided to Sadler, in 1904, by the new LEA. The subscription list for 'the Building Fund and Jubilee Extension' amounted to just over £20,000, but more than half as much again was otherwise raised. In today's terms, about £1.5m of privately-donated money was spent on building both phases of what today is called The Ramsden Building, and the total layout on its construction was about £2.8m.
13. *Calendars* for 1895-6, p.95; 1902-03, p.229.
14. *Calendars* for 1898-9, p.169; 1900-01, pp.239-40; 1902-3, p.273; 1903-04, p.242.
15. *Calendar for 1901-02*, p.250; p.215 *et. seq.*
16. Sadler later became Vice-Chancellor of Leeds University and then Master of University College, Oxford (*DNB*).
17. *Calendar for 1904-05*, p.252.
18. Sadler Report, pp.70-101, 125-6.
19. *Calendar for 1906-7*, 41, pp.247-8.
20. *Calendars* for 1905-06, pp.234-8; 1906-07, p.247.
21. Sadler Report, pp.70-71; *Calendars* for 1904-05, pp.262-4; 1906-07, p.245; 1907-08, pp.250-2.
22. *Calendars* for 1906-07, p.236; 1908-09, pp.264-5.
23. *Calendar for 1908-09*, p.2; 'Report on the Technical and Evening Schools in the County Borough of Huddersfield for the period ending 31 July 1909' (1909).
24. *Calendar for … 1909-10*, pp.268-9.
25. *Calendar for … 1910-11*, pp.vii-x.
26. *Calendars* for 1912-13, p.276; 1911-12, p.264.
27. *Calendar for the 73rd Session, 1913-14*, pp.392-3. The museum had been established in 1885, when the new Technical School and Mechanics' Institute took over the collection of the Huddersfield Literary and Scientific Society. See E A Hilary Haigh, ed. *Huddersfield A Most Handsome Town. Aspects of the history and culture of a West Yorkshire Town* (Huddersfield 1992), p.684 *et seq.*

CHAPTER 4

IV. St. Paul's interior

CHAPTER 4

WAR AND PEACE, 1914-46

(a) The First World War and its Aftermath, 1914-24

The 1914-18 war was a stimulus to, rather than a brake upon, the growth of the College. Though over 200 students immediately enlisted, the decrease in teaching hours in the 1914-15 session was of less than one per cent. Apart from special courses for women 'on short time', and then to train women 'to replace men' in clerical and commercial employment, there was no diversion of the College from its normal development.[1] Most striking about the war years is the little disruption to staff. Only two are mentioned as having served in the Forces: Dr H D C Lee and Mr H Topping.* The numbers of College Diplomas and Certificates awarded fell significantly in the war years, but there were war-time stimulants to development, too, the most important being the creation, in 1916, of a Coal Tar Colour Chemistry Department, as a result of the formation of British Dyes Ltd, and of the asserted German near-monopoly of this branch of Chemistry.[2] Mr J Turner, an ex-student - later to be Sir Joseph Turner and a College governor for 24 years - had been Chairman of Read Holliday, the Huddersfield chemical firm which, on government orders, had joined with Levinstein's, of Manchester, to form British Dyes in 1915. He now promised that British Dyes would make a substantial contribution towards the establishment of the new department. Sir John Ramsden continued his family's tradition of munificent support to the institution with a donation of £3,000 in 1917, £2,000 intended for the Colour Chemistry Department and £1,000 for Engineering.[3] This was in response to a large-scale organisation of Aldermen and Councillors of the Borough, led by Alderman Joseph Blamires, also a former student, and a prominent benefactor, to canvass individuals and associations in order to raise money for extension funds to benefit the Colour Chemistry, Textile and Engineering Departments, and for a 'general fund'.[4] These funds were raised - in an atmosphere of war-time patriotism - because the Board of Education did not contribute to the cost of new building for technical education, and support from local rates was limited to 3d in the £ (ie 3/240ths).[5]

When war broke out, the Governors' concern had been to build a new Textile Department. During the war, other needs accumulated, of Engineering, Dyeing and Art. But Colour Chemistry was the fashionable department. In May 1916 a Head of Department, Dr A E Everest, was appointed, and in December the Governors resolved that an 'extension' to house the department should be the first building project undertaken, and that 'as soon as possible'. A deputation to promote this scheme was favourably received, in March 1917, by the President of the Board of Education, the famous historian, H A L Fisher. There was a renewed appeal for funds in November 1917, specifically for this department. But in December, the Governors, pressed by the Council's Education Committee, accepted that the Board be approached 'for provisional recognition of' the 'premises' that had been designated to Colour Chemistry 'as a Junior

---

*   Dr Lee had been appointed Lecturer and Head of French in 1912. An Army Captain, he was blinded in 1918. The Governors hoped he would resume teaching in September 1919, after training in braille. That same month, December 1918, the first national salary scale was introduced. It was revised in July 1919, when many salaries rose from £220 to £350, and some from £290 to £450. Dr Lee's remained fixed at the £250 he had been appointed to in 1912. He did resume his post, and was promoted to Senior Lecturer in 1934; he retired in 1944. Lance-Corporal Topping, who had been Thomas Thorp's Assistant Secretary, was killed in action on 22 April 1918.[1]

Technical School'. In April 1918 the Governors resolved to 'form a Research Association' 'in connection with the Privy Council scheme for Scientific and Industrial Research', and in the meantime to postpone the formation of 'a separate fund' for the Department of Colour Chemistry. In July the Board of Education approved the Junior Technical School proposal as 'a useful step in the development of a complete system of higher education for the County Borough of Huddersfield'. Left with only the prospect of a research fund of £4,500 from the total of £15,000 which had been donated to Colour Chemistry, Dr Everest had resigned, in June. He was replaced within two months by Dr H H Hodgson, 'of Bradford'. In Dr Everest, the College lost a distinguished scientist.* Yet the foundation of the future distinction of the College in chemical research was laid in this episode. The research fund was to be the means of financing scholarships that were to help sustain the research reputation built by Dr Hodgson between the wars. It was added to in 1920, when Alderman Blamires's widow donated £2,000 'for scholarships … in Chemical Research …' in his memory, and a British Dyes Research Scholarship fund, worth £150 a year, was instituted.[6]

But after the war it was the longer-standing accommodation needs of the Textile and Dyeing Departments that were given priority. The generous gifts of textile employers' associations in the Huddersfield district and the patient acquisition of buildings opposite the College on Queen Street South culminated in the approval of a building scheme by the employers, and their conveyance of the land and accumulated funds to the Corporation, as a gift.[7] The new Textiles Building, on the corner of Princess Street, was formally opened on 26 October 1920 by Lord Askwith.[8] The whole conversion and fitting operation cost £50,000, of which the Corporation contributed only £6,500. At the same time, the Dyeing Department was provided with a new dyehouse and laboratories, at a cost of £4,000. The plan to build a Junior Technical School on the land adjacent to the College that had been designated for a Coal Tar Colour Chemistry building was replaced in July 1920 by a scheme to build a 'new Technical College and joint Secondary School' on the site of the 'College Municipal Secondary School' for boys (Huddersfield College) at Highfields, New North Road. But the climate changed: the Fisher Education Act of 1918 had made part-time day-continuation schooling compulsory, but by the end of 1922 the Act was a dead letter. In the post-war economic slump, the 'Geddes Axe' had fallen on government expenditure.[9] The Huddersfield scheme was just one that it cut off.

Nominally presiding, as Chairman of the Governors, over the later-wartime negotiations for building extensions was John Arthur Brooke. His older brother, Thomas, President from 1879 to 1886, had been the driving force behind the building of the new Technical School. Thomas had been created baronet in 1899, and died in 1908. John Arthur had taken over from him as President, had been succeeded in 1890 by John Fligg Brigg, then succeeded him, in September 1899, just before Brigg died. Thus, from 1877 to 1919, a Brooke or a Brigg was President, or, after 1903, Chairman of

22. Sir John Arthur Brooke

---

* He went to University College, Reading, where he became Professor of Chemistry.

Governors. In the first post-war Honours List, of June 1919, in which John Arthur was created baronet, Dr Michael Sadler was also knighted, and the College Governors sent congratulations to both, for by now Sir John was a sick man. He resigned the Chairmanship from November, and the Governors resolved that the office of President be revived and that he be invited to accept it. Lady Brooke replied, on 23 December 1919, to convey her husband's thanks, but his regret that he was unable to accept 'in his present state of health'. He died in July 1920, and his death marked the end of an era more than merely chronologically. He was 76, and was one of the last of the generations of men who - like his father, John Brooke, in the 1850s and 1860s - had worked and paid for the Mechanics' Institution.

23. Sir Thomas Brooke

There were changes and attempted changes in the aftermath of war. Under the Fisher Act, teacher training in the College came to an end in 1920, though the Governors tried to persuade the Board of Education to make it a centre for training ex-service men as teachers.[10] Another new management arrangement came into force in 1921, also as required by the Act: the Council's functions in relation to the College were taken over by the Education Committee, and the College Board of Governors became one of its Sub-committees. In its re-constitution, representation of the City and Guilds of London Institute (CGLI) was ended.[11] The College's museum, which had been associated with the Pupil Teacher Centre, was transferred to 'Ravensknowle' after the gift to the Council of his house and grounds by Legh Tolson, to commemorate the deaths in the war of his two nephews[12] Thus was begun the Tolson Memorial Museum in Ravensknowle Park. There was a post-war expansion in student numbers, particularly in the area of non-vocational adult classes, and a new department, Humanistic Studies, which embraced this area, was formed in 1919.[13]

In this atmosphere of expansion, the possibility was raised for the third time of enhancing the status of the College. Pressure came from the recently-formed Board of Studies, made up of Heads of Departments, who were encouraged to make the move by a Board of Education report on the College. In 1922 the College underwent an inspection on a scale that was not to be repeated for 30 years, and that was to be looked back on then as a landmark. It lasted for a month, and when the confidential report was received, in December, the Governors set up two sub-committees: one to consider each departmental report and decide what action it called for; the other 'to consider what steps can be taken to raise and improve the status of the College'. The LEA was persuaded to approach Leeds University with a suggestion that Huddersfield should become a college of the university. The University's Council met specifically to consider this proposal in October 1923, and a deputation visited the College. The negotiations dragged on till 1928. Dr

24. Tolson Museum

Baillie, the Vice-Chancellor, offered an 'amended' 'affiliation status', which, however, was unacceptable to the College. The correspondence became acrimonious. At one point, a worried Dr Baillie withdrew a letter he had written and asked for its return. The Governors pressed for the Authority's annual grant to the University to be withdrawn, but diplomacy sufficiently prevailed for a reduced grant to be paid, and for the University to retain its representation on the Council's Education Committee.[14]

A notable feature of these negotiations is that Mr Hudson appears to have taken no part. During some of this time he was lying low, and perhaps was even *persona non grata*. From late 1923, a Governors' 'Small Classes Sub-Committee', having decreed a norm of 'actual teaching (of) not less than 20 hours per week', scrutinised departments in what to the staff must have felt like a reign of terror. The Principal was reprimanded for having 'failed to carry out ... resolutions'. Thereafter, the Director of Education carried them out. In July two members of the Humanities staff resigned, and the department's new Head left 'as from 31 December 1924', when the post-inspection scrutiny was still going on.[15]

(b) Between the Wars, 1918-39

The most constructive development nationally in technical education after 1918 was the inception of National Certificates and Diplomas, awarded on part-time and full-time courses, respectively. These were joint awards of the Board of Education and professional bodies, made at Ordinary (ONC, OND) and Higher (HNC, HND) levels. The first awards were made in Chemistry, Applied Chemistry and Mechanical Engineering. The College began teaching for these schemes in 1921-2, and its first awards were made in 1923.[16] By then the subject range had been widened to include Textiles, Commerce and Building. The College's own Diplomas and Certificates continued to be awarded, and to them were added, in March 1923, the College Associateship, which required holders of the HND or an accepted equivalent to complete an additional year's relevant work experience and submit a dissertation on an approved related topic. This award was sparingly given, and usually to holders of doctorates.[17]

25. Student on a loom

The inter-war period was not a creative one for technical education, but within rigid limits set by a national climate of near-stagnation and its being controlled by an LEA which did not complete the building of a single school in the period, Huddersfield Technical College did remarkably well. The economic depression of the 1920s and early 1930s is evident in provision for admission to classes, without charge, of 'suitable unemployed or partially employed young persons', in suggestions of special day classes for older men and women, and in the holding of free classes for unemployed secondary-school (selective, 'grammar' school) leavers, and of free workshop classes for unemployed engineers.[18] But after slightly falling from a peak of 3,900 in 1923-4, student numbers rose steadily from 1924-5 to 1938-9, when the total was 4,379. There was almost no change, though, in the percentage of full-time students in the total, which remained at about ten, and almost 80 per cent were evening-only students. The expansion was evenly spread, and was in modern languages, history and geography, and domestic economy, as well as in science and technology. Nor was there discernible change in the college's level of work. Ten students were awarded external PhDs between 1928 and 1939, all in Chemistry, and the highest number awarded in any one year was three. In 1928 the regulations for the College Associateship were tightened, to make a first degree, followed by work experience and two years' advanced study at the College pre-conditions. To the 16 Associateships awarded between 1923 and 1934 only three more were added before 1939. Numbers of students working for first degrees rose slightly in the 1930s. The number of awards in 1938-9 is fairly representative: one MSc degree; four final honours, in Science and Arts; eight intermediate degrees in Science and three in Commerce; and three Intermediate BSc (Engineering) degrees. At a lower level were London Matriculation successes, between 10 and 20 per year; and external examinations for professional qualifications. These included the intermediate examinations for the RIBA, pharmaceutical, Institute of Bankers, and accountancy and secretarial qualifications. In 1939 there were six awards of Higher National Diploma, 14 Higher

26. Alderman Albert Hirst

National Certificates and 45 Ordinary Nationals, across Engineering, Chemistry and Building. The College awarded its own diplomas and certificates, at a lower level, in these subjects plus Dyeing; about 30 in each were given annually in the 1930s. The mass numbers of examination passes were still in the 'City and Guilds' and the now Royal Society of Arts examinations: in the mid-1920s they totalled about 325; in the 1930s about 450 annually. Hundreds of students were not examined. Mr Hudson was not given to rhetoric, but his last report, in 1937, described the institution in the words of a prophet: as 'a Regional College', a 'University of the people', 'a local centre for advanced study and research in artistic, literary and historical, scientific and technological' subjects. The next year's report, the first of Dr J W Whitaker, claimed a 'significant movement' toward 'day-time instruction' - though it is difficult to see on what evidence - and made a plea for more day release of students, condemning the drawbacks of evening classes in tones reminiscent of Dr Rawson more than 30 years before.[19]

By the later 1930s the College was bursting at the seams. It occupied eight separate buildings - the Building Department alone was housed in six - and, for 10 years, the Principal's reports had sung a litany of complaint about lack of space and overcrowding.[20] There had been some improvements to the engineering laboratories after the war, and in 1924 a grant of £3,500 from the Miners' Welfare Fund, which, after an embarrassing delay, was used to equip a laboratory for the teaching of mining. The 'Coal Tar Colour Chemistry Fund' that had been raised from 'industry and other well-wishers' in 1916-18 re-appeared on the Governors' agenda in 1924 as the 'Huddersfield Technical College Extension Fund'. The money accumulated was now £18,000, and to that was to be added £2,000 of accrued interest. In 1929 subscribers were 'asked to allow their donations to be used for any new building for Advanced Study and research in Chemistry'.[21] The Town Council approved building plans for 'new Chemical Laboratories', but its Finance Committee blocked the expenditure, and the Principal was reduced to calling for 'a generous benefactor who will invest in the future'. Perhaps some donors thought they already had. Hope was re-kindled; building work began in 1936, and the foundation stone of this largely privately-financed building was laid on 2 July 1937 by Alderman Albert Hirst, Chairman of the Governors. The long-awaited relief to be given by the new 'extension' was postponed at the outbreak of war in September 1939, when the government commandeered the more-or-less complete building. An official opening, planned for May 1940, was put off 'owing to grave war developments', but the College took over the building. Even then, as had been realised in 1937, a further extension was needed to provide the College with 'the more dignified accommodation it deserves', and the out-lying buildings still had to be used.[22]

Academically, the status of the College was raised, and its research reputation established, in the inter-war years. It had the funds, through its 'Joseph Blamires' and 'British Dyes' scholarships and other endowments, and from grants from the Department of Scientific and Industrial Research (DSIR), to recruit up to 10 full-time graduate research students. Annual lists of staff publications were dominated by the research papers produced by the Coal Tar Colour Chemistry Department, but staff across the departments had publications to their credit.[23] Consistently with this academic advance, there was some improvement in the College's library services. Mr Hudson deliberately cultivated a collegiate spirit and an academic atmosphere.

27. Dr J W Whitaker

Student facilities improved, and activities expanded: sporting clubs were formed, a dramatic society flourished, a student magazine, *Mock Turtle*, was launched; and an Appointments Board was set up to advise full-time students.[24] A Students' Representative Council was elected from 1930, and in the acute depression years, 1930 and 1931, it organised charitable activities. Student drama 'prospered exceedingly'. A group called 'The Social Service Players' won two 'highly commended' awards at a Drama League festival in 1936. In 1934 there were extensive 'Golden Jubilee' celebrations of '50 years of technical education'. The main events were crowded into a September week-end, when the guest speakers were a former Economics lecturer in the College, Arthur Greenwood, Minister of Health in the Labour government of 1929-31 and future member of Churchill's War Cabinet, and Phyllis Bentley, the novelist and local celebrity; and the Bishop of Wakefield preached at a Jubilee service in the Parish Church.[25]

An important development regionally was the formation of the Yorkshire Council for Further Education (YCFE). Characteristically, the Huddersfield Education Authority refused annual invitations to join it - because of the subscriptions involved - till 1937.[26] 'Further Education' was an elastic term, as was illustrated when, in 1938, a scheme was introduced to send apprentices to FE colleges for one day a week. Dr Whitaker welcomed the idea, as a revival of the 'day continuation schools' provided for in the 1918 Education Act that had been cut off by the Geddes Axe. He called it 'the righting of one of the great social tragedies of our time'. The outbreak of war in 1939 caused the postponement of the raising of the school-leaving age to 15, as had been provided for in the 1936 Education Act. Dr Whitaker was enthusiastic about these 'junior employees' of 14 and 15 being in the College - which had supposedly set a minimum age of entry of 16 in 1914 - because it would repair 'the weakest link in FE: that immediately following school leaving'. He was, presumably, not a close-enough student of the College's history to know that the Sadler Report of 1904 had recommended the ending of this 'continuation school' function of the College, and that Dr Rawson had campaigned for the raising of the age, and thus the standard, of entry before that. He was as pleased as Dr Rawson would have been, though, to record in this report for 1938 that George Kaye, the College's external graduate of 1902, had been elected Fellow of the Royal Society.[27]

(c) The Second World War, 1939-46

In contrast with 1914-15, there was a drastic fall in student numbers in 1939-40. Thereafter, they rose steadily, and in 1944-45 there were nearly 5,000, the most ever. Because of the reserved-occupation system, numbers were low in the Textiles and Dyeing departments but little affected in science and engineering, and Chemical Engineering, a 'new venture', 'received excellent support'. New forms of record inform about the student composition: two-thirds were Borough residents; nearly all the rest were from the neighbouring West Riding. In 1943, 50 per cent had attended elementary schools (often followed by attendance at evening institutes), 10 per cent were from (selective) central schools and 40 per cent from secondary (grammar) schools. As well as its own students, the College contrived to accommodate a variety of guests. From 1941, 300 women students of Avery Hill Teacher Training College, evacuated, with 30 staff, from Eltham, south-east London, occupied part of the 'New Extension', for 'the duration'. Classes of soldiers, training to be radio mechanics; members of the women's ATS, who were taking a commercial course; REME fitters, who took up the space left when the radio-mechanic classes ended; and engineering-officer cadets from all the services were taught in the College. From 10pm to 6am, there were 'crash' training schemes for civilians in bench skills.[28] 'Normal' developments which the war allowed included large-scale revisions of the National Certificate curricula in Chemistry, Engineering and Commerce. There was, again, little disruption of the staffing of the College: only five men on the teaching staff were in the Forces in late 1944 from a total

28. Chemistry Building, Queen Street South, (now Queensgate) – opened in 1940

of 75 full-time members, who were supplemented by 250 part-timers. Though by the end of the war there were staffing shortages, output of research and publications did not much decline; and student social and cultural activities blossomed, not least because of the presence of the Avery Hill women students.[29]

Debate on 'post-war reconstruction' went on in government from mid-1940. Its most-renowned emanation was the 1942 'Beveridge Report'.[30] The contentiousness and projected cost of Beveridge's proposals for the extension of 'social insurance' explain why educational reform was given precedence. R A Butler's Education Act thus became the great war-time social reform. A White Paper of July 1943, *Educational Reconstruction*, proposed only meagre financial provision for technical and other further education. Butler, President of the Board of Education, had seemed well disposed, and his White Paper did acknowledge the contribution of technical colleges to war-time training needs, and lament the poor buildings and equipment common in the colleges. There was, too, a vigorous supportive campaign: in Parliament; and outside, by educationalists and industrialists. But in March 1944 Butler funnelled off technical education to a committee under the chairmanship of Lord Eustace Percy - author of a highly-regarded book on the subject, *Education at the Crossroads*, published in 1931 - and the Percy Report, on *Higher Technical Education*, was not issued till 1945. Consequently, the Education Act of August 1944 made no direct reference to vocational education. It merely laid on Local Education Authorities the duty - whereas before they had had the option - to submit to the new Ministry of Education development schemes for providing 'adequate facilities for further education'.[31] As with the 'continuation schools' provision of the 1918 Act, the requirement of compulsory part-time education to age 18 in the 1944 Act was never implemented. In this connection, Dr Whitaker's eve-of-war enthusiasm for the prospect of 'junior employees' in the College had been destroyed by the experience. By the time he resigned, in March 1946 - to become Director of an Indian fuel-research institute - he was convinced they were a 'pernicious influence' and that their presence was 'against the spirit' of the new Act.[32]

Notes on Chapter 4

1. Huddersfield County Borough Council (HCBC). Proceedings of the Education Committee (Proc Educ Comm), 1923-4, 91; Technical and Further Education Sub-Committee (Tech and FE S-C) 14.3.24, 3.7.44; Principal's Report (PR) for 1943-4; Proc Counc November 1918-October 1919, p.216, pp.477-9; November 1917-October 1918, p.315.
2. HCBC Proc Counc: Mins of Tech Coll Govs, 22 February 1916; 2 Feb 1916.
3. Tech Coll Govs: Textile S-C, 6 June 1916; Extensions S-C, 26 June 1916.
4. *Ibid*, 26 February 1917.
5. Application to the Local Government Board: Govs mins, 27 February 1919.
6. Proc Counc, November 1917-October 1918, pp.47, 97, 230, 275, 349, 358, 393, 395, 441, 442, 443; November 1918-October 1919, p.376; November 1919-October 1920, p.310.
7. Govs mins, 24 September 1918; 17 December 1918, confirmed by Council, 18 December 1918.
8. Not to be confused with Herbert Henry Asquith, Liberal Prime Minister, 1908-16, created Earl of Oxford and Asquith in 1925, who, however, had a family connection with the College. He was born in Morley, near Leeds, in 1852, and, after his father's death, in 1861, his mother brought her four children to live near the house, in Trinity Street, Huddersfield, of her father, William Willans, a substantial woolstapler and a supporter and Director of the Mechanics' Institution for over 20 years till his death in 1863. His eldest son, J E Willans, Asquith's uncle, who married the daughter of Edward Baines, MP for Leeds 1859-74 and proprietor of the *Leeds Mercury*, was equally supportive. These families belonged to the Congregationalist élite prominent in West Riding towns.
9. Govs mins 28 September 1920; Tech Coll S-C, 21 February 1922; Govs mins 18 December 1917, 23 July 1918; 27 July 1920.
   When the post-war boom burst, Sir Eric Geddes, Minister of Transport, was appointed chairman of a committee on government expenditure. Education was the chief victim of the economies that followed from the committee's recommendations of February 1922.
10. Govs mins 27 February 1919; S-C, 2 December 1920, 28 February 1921.
11. Govs mins 25 November 1919; 24 February 1920; 28 June 1921; Tech Coll S-C 29 November 1920; 4 and 29 May 1922.
12. Proc Counc: General Purposes Committee, 8 May 1919; Govs mins 24 February 1920.
13. Govs mins, 27 May, 2, 24 June; 9 July, 23 December 1919.
14. Tech Coll S-C, 26 September 1922; Tech and FE S-C, 18 and 19 December 1922; 14 February, 26 June, 24 July 1923; Departmental Report to the Mayor 1924. HCB Educ Comm Mins, 1925-6 to 1927-8, *passim*; 1932-3, 103. Sir Michael Sadler left Leeds for Oxford in 1923.
15. HCB: Proc of Educ Comm, November 1923-October 1924, pp.53-4, 91-2, 110-111, 129-30, 152-3, 178, 181, 204; November 1924-October 1925, 17, p.207.
16. Proc Counc: Tech Coll S-C, 20 December 1921; 24 January 1922.
17. Tech and FE S-C, 27 March 1923. Sixteen awards had been made by 1934 (Huddersfield Technical College, PR for 1933-4, p.1).
18. Tech and FE S-C, 14 February 1923; PR for 1930-31; Departmental Reports to the Mayor 1931-2, 1932-3.
19. PR; Departmental Reports to the Mayor, *passim*.
20. PR, 1927-8, 1928-9, etc.
21. HCBC Educ Comm: Tech and FE S-C, 17.12.29, 24.6.30.
22. PR 1932-3, p.(viii); 1935-6, p.(ix); 1936-7, p.6; 1938-9, p.9; 1939-40, p.5.
23. Eg, PR, 1928-9, p.(v); 1931-32, Appendix II; 1932-33, Appendix II.
24. *Cf* PR, 1933-34, p.(v); 1938-39, p.14; 1931-32, p.(viii); 1933-34, p.(vii); 1935-6, p.(ix); 1932-33, p.(viii).
25. CBH 'Technical College Jubilee, 1884-1934' (1934); Departmental Report to the Mayor, 1936-37. Greenwood, Deputy Leader of the Labour Party, was Minister without Portfolio in Churchill's War Cabinet of five from its formation in May 1940 to February 1942.
26. HCBC: Proc of Educ Comm, 1928-9, 819, 1184; Tech and FE S-C, 1934-5, 1936-7.
27. PR 1938-39, p.7; *Calendar for 1898-99*, p.147; *Calendar for 1902-3*, p.165.
28. PR 1939-40 to 1944-45 *passim*; PR 1943-44, p.10.
29. PR 1940-41, p.1; 1944-45, p.6.
30. *Report on Social Insurance and Allied Services*, 20 November 1942. Cmd. 6404.
31. J Stuart Maclure, *Educational Documents*, 4th ed (1979), pp.206-9; PR 1942-3, 1944-5; *Educational Reconstruction*, July 1944, CMD. 6458. Percy had been President of the Board of Education in Baldwin's government of 1924-9.
32. PR 1944-45, p.2.

CHAPTER 5

V. Architectural detail, Ramsden Building

CHAPTER 5

THE SCOTT ERA, 1946-70

(a) A Decade of Uncertainty, 1946-56

For ten years after the war there was uncertainty and uneven expansion in further and higher education. The Percy Report warned of an impending shortage of scientists and technologists, and recommended an overall strategy for 'trained manpower'. The Barlow Committee, reporting in 1946 on *Scientific Manpower*, called for a doubling of the output of scientists in the next ten years. There were impressive-looking achievements. The Barlow target of a doubling of science places in universities was reached by 1947. The number of full-time students of technology at degree level 'or equivalent' in 1949-50, nearly 11,000, was double that in 1938-9. In 1955, 9,500 qualified on 'advanced' courses in technical colleges in England and Wales. The number of day-release students, 42,000 in 1938-9, was over 350,000 in 1954-5.[1]

But there were factors retarding expansion. The Labour governments of 1945-51, facing financial crises in 1947 and 1949, and the costs of the emerging Cold War and of the rearmament consequent on the outbreak of the Korean war in 1950, concentrated educational expenditure on the schools. There were conflicts of interest among the parties involved in further and higher education. The Barlow Committee had assumed that its called-for doubling of the output of scientists would take place solely in the universities, and daringly suggested that there was enough intelligence in an age group to justify increasing the number going to university from one per cent to five. Even the reputedly expansionist/egalitarian Percy Report had drawn the class distinctions of scientists in the universities, technologists in senior colleges and technicians in the rest. Only university students were awarded degrees: college technologists received diplomas from external awarding bodies; and professional qualifications were the guarded preserve of the engineering institutions. It was a system, as *The Times Educational Supplement* described it, of 'the universities taking the high road and the technical colleges the low'. The Barlow Report had distinguished between the technology taught in universities and that taught in technical colleges, and a 'Note on technology in the Universities' issued by the University Grants Committee (UGC) in 1950 distinguished it from technology in the colleges as 'a difference ... not in status or grade but in kind'. The distinction 'ought to be recognised more clearly in planning future change'.[2] Such views were the rationale behind what was to become known as 'the binary system'. It was still to be a system of higher and lower prestige, but it signified a rise in status for those technical colleges that came within the system, in that they were in a 'higher education' hemisphere, albeit the lower half. Universities, though increasingly financed publicly, via the UGC, were private institutions. Technical colleges were in the further education sector of the public education service, controlled by their LEAs.

In the College, the presence of Dr Whitaker's 'junior employees' was one of the items on the first agenda of the new Principal, Dr W E Scott - also a chemist - who took up his post in September 1946. When he condemned the 'mixture of Junior and Senior Students', which he thought was bad for both, he was aware that Sir Michael Sadler had done that 40 years before, and that Dr Rawson had before that. But the 'junior industrial course' remained his problem till 1948. The other main items on Dr Scott's list were issues raised in the plethora of post-war education reports, Ministry circulars and administrative memoranda, and the problem of inadequate accommodation, made more acute because student numbers rose precipitately in the immediate post-war years. The 'many official publications' all made sound recommendations, he thought, but experience showed that staff of the right quality were not attracted to the colleges: salary scales did not compare with those of university teachers, or with those in industry.[3] The College's problems, like its work, covered the whole range of further and higher education. At the same time as short 'post-graduate' courses were being developed, the steady increase in day release had, by 1953, brought to over 2,000 the number attending these courses, 700 more than in 1946-7. But the balance was wrong. In this first post-war decade, if the academic composition of the student body changed at all, it was towards reducing the proportion of higher-level work within it.[4] Dr Scott complained that the machinery of national and regional councils set up for further education was not working, and that the prestige of university degrees was inhibiting the development of full-time courses for higher technological awards, so that universities, with their 'splendid new buildings' going up, were expanding, but, at advanced levels, the technical colleges were not. Even if the universities doubled their numbers, argued Dr Scott, 'there is evidence that there is another group of 5-10 per cent of the population who would benefit from another type of higher education' (thereby tacitly accepting the UGC's case for 'difference … in kind'). He feared that trouble was being built up, too, because, though the number of science students in universities had doubled by 1952, the number of science teachers in schools was declining. 'The position in the feeding ground' must be improved. 'The big educational problem' was 'how to attract the right staff into the classroom'. He told senior staff in 1952 that students 'should be persuaded to take a scientific or technological course' to help meet the national shortage, and, prompted by the British Association's meeting in Leeds on that theme, he was still saying so in 1967.[5]

30. Dr W E Scott

Overall, the College's numbers rose relentlessly: in 1945-6 there had been over 5,000 students registered; by 1948-9 there were 6,400; then, after a slow-down, 7,000 in 1953-4, when another upward trend set in. From the first, Dr Scott had predicted that there would have to be 'a several-storeyed building on the site behind the new extension', but alternatives were explored and interim solutions sought. In 1948 a plan was approved for a new refectory to replace the war-time canteen that held 60, when the average daily student attendance was over 800; but no start had been made at the end of 1950. There was no staff common room: the only staff room there was was used for meals, and was packed when 30 were seated; in the evenings it was a classroom. The accommodation for Architecture lacked any heating, and had a leaking roof.[6] Belatedly, a pre-fabricated Domestic Science and Catering Building came into use in 1950, but the needs of Textiles and other departments remained unmet, and by 1953 'saturation point' had been reached.[7] In 1949 a 'draft building development plan' had been approved. Nothing had been done to implement it when the first 'full general inspection' for 30 years was carried out in 1952, and inevitably accommodation deficiencies were criticised. After many delays and averred searchings for alternative sites, it was concluded 'that there was no ... alternative to ... developing the College in its present position'. Following a public enquiry, and in a highly-charged debate - because of the housing clearance involved - the Town Council, in February 1954, divided 28 votes to 23 in favour of issuing a compulsory purchase order.[8]

Despite the difficulties, there were major academic initiatives in these post-war years. The nascent 'Huddersfield Technical (Teachers') Training College', which was later to grow on the Holly Bank campus and in 1974 to merge with the Polytechnic, began its life in the Technical College in 1947.[9] Within the College, and building on the tradition of singing classes through most of its history, the foundations of a Music department were laid in September 1948 by the appointment of a full-time lecturer. Initially, Dr Scott reported, like her 'sister', 'Dramatic Art', Music was 'rightly placed within Humanistic Studies'. The first orchestral concert was given in December 1950, when also was begun what became the tradition of the Christmas Festival of Nine Lessons and Carols held in St Paul's Church; and there were concerts to celebrate the College's 110th anniversary, in March 1951, when an Exhibition, which 15,000 people visited, was timed to coincide with the Festival of Britain.[10] Another anniversary exhibition was held in March 1956, and a few days before it opened, Sir David Eccles, Conservative Minister of Education, presented to Parliament his long-awaited White Paper, *Technical Education*. The omens had been contradictory for Huddersfield. In 1953-4, Chemistry had been approved as a course to which the increased student grant - raised, under a Ministry Circular of 1952 from 60 to 75 per cent of university grants - applied. But the applications of Textiles and Engineering had been rejected; and in 1954-5 the Ministry had asked for Governors to consider closing some full-time degree and diploma courses, because of the small

31. Chemistry students in the 1940s

numbers recruited.[11] Nationally, of the limited expansion of higher technological education since 1945, the universities had been the main beneficiaries, and Dr Scott had complained in 1953 that the role of technical colleges was still not clear.[12] The new White Paper was to open a period - punctuated by the publication of further White Papers in 1961, 1966 and 1972, and of the Robbins Report on Higher Education, in 1963 - of rapid expansion, during which priority came to be given to technical colleges, and there was established that 'binary system', of spreading higher education across the university and LEA-controlled public sectors.[13]

(b) The Halting Progression to Polytechnic Status, 1956-70

1956 was an uplifting year for Huddersfield. It was named in the Eccles White Paper as one of 24 institutions which might become Colleges of Advanced Technology (CATs) that were to teach exclusively advanced courses, mainly in full-time and 'sandwich' (including work experience) modes, and the Principal's only apparent worries were the continuous accommodation and staffing problems. But in 1957 there was the disappointment of Bradford's selection, over Huddersfield, as a CAT, and in July 1958, though sandwich courses in Chemical Technology and Dyeing were approved by the new validating body, the National Council for Technological Awards (NCTA), applications in Mechanical and Electrical Engineering were rejected. Worse was to come. 'Pressure from Regional influences' resulted in the removal of the Dyeing course to Bradford and the cessation of all teaching for London University's external degrees, in spite of the Governors' appeal to the Minister not to allow the ending of a 60-year tradition. In 1958 the Regional Council (YCFE) recommended that Chemistry and related subjects should no longer be offered at the newly-renamed Huddersfield Regional College of Technology.[14] But the nadir was reached in 1962, when the NCTA did not renew approval for the College's only Diploma in Technology (DipTech) course, in Chemistry. Desperately, Governors, Education Committee and Town Council fought to combat a suggestion from the Ministry that 'Regional College' status should be withdrawn. A reprieve was granted, and, as Dr Scott reported, 'we retain our position as a Regional College at least until the Robbins Committee reports'.[15] The Principal's advice of April 1956 had been ignored, and he was entitled to castigate the Authority for its failure to implement an adequate building programme - which the government would have subsidised - and to 'separate out the more elementary work'. Doing that had been a condition of the NCTA's original approval, and its fulfilment would have allowed the College to concentrate on the recruitment of advanced students. Hastily, late in 1962, the LEA submitted a scheme to the Ministry for the establishment of a 'Branch College' to take the lower-level work.[16]

32. Anthony Crosland, Secretary of State for Education and Science, 1965-67

An Education Act of 1962 incorporated the recommendation of the Anderton Committee that LEAs should be compelled to finance equally all full-time students on courses requiring a two-or-more GCE A-Level entry. The Robbins Report of late 1963 enunciated the 'principle' '… that courses of higher education should be available for all those who are qualified by ability and attainment to pursue them and who wish to do so'. The consequence of the government's acceptance of this principle, for student numbers and future costs of higher education, were to be enormous. It meant an immediate commitment to a ten-year programme costing £3.5bn, when total annual public expenditure was £11 bn. The Report envisaged an increase in full-time student numbers from 216,000 in 1962-3 to 560,000 by 1980-81. The CATs were to become technological universities, and the NCTA was to be replaced by the Council for National Academic Awards (CNAA), whose charter allowed it to approve degree proposals from colleges over a much wider academic range than the technologies supervised by the NCTA. The Robbins Committee did not favour higher education outside universities, but accepted the fact that it was there. The consequences of its Report were doubly ironical: whereas the Committee envisaged the expansion it planned would be mainly in science and technology, and mainly in the universities, the increased numbers were to be mainly in arts, business studies and social studies, and largely outside the universities.

The Labour government that came to power in 1964 accepted the Robbins expansion but rejected the Robbins strategy of concentrating degree-level work in the universities and regarding the Regional Colleges rather as an overspill. Anthony Crosland, the new Secretary of State for Education and Science, confirmed the binary system as the principled basis of government policy. His 1966 White Paper, *A Plan for Polytechnics and Other Colleges*, aimed to concentrate degree-level work in the public sector into a limited number of colleges. Thirty polytechnics were eventually designated, but the CNAA came to authorise such courses in many 'other colleges'. The vast increase in the number of mainly non-science and non-technology students outside the universities took place because the Treasury had failed to set an overall limit on polytechnic funding. The higher-education 'pool' provided for by the 1958 Local Government Act was, in the jargon, an 'open pool', with no limit on it.

The 'Branch College', named 'Ramsden Technical College', was established in 1963 within the College of Technology's buildings, and its first Principal, appointed for a three-year term, was Dr Bosley, who remained Vice-Principal of the 'senior' College. The paper transfer of 4,165 'junior students' - from 10,000 totally - gave no relief from accommodation

33. Alderman John L Dawson

pressures, and the 'evolutionary manner' of the separation was to go on till 1980. But this was a symbolic end to the local-college function,[*][17] and when the Robbins Report was issued, in October, the tide was turning for the College's fortunes. Even so, the process of gaining the CNAA's approval to teach College-devised schemes was an obstacle course. HM Inspectors advised the Regional Councils and the Department of Education and Science (DES), which had to approve the adequacy of resources and the likelihood of recruitment; and the CNAA's role was to assess the academic soundness of proposals and the adequacy of staff support. In 1964-5 the CNAA approved honours-degree proposals in Chemical Technology and Electrical Engineering at Huddersfield, but a submission in Mechanical Engineering was rejected.[18] The 125th anniversary celebrations of the College's foundation were held in March-April 1966 in an atmosphere of high optimism. They were attended by Ms Ismena Holland, granddaughter of Frederic Schwann, who marked the occasion by endowing the College with a Foundation Scholarship, the value of which she later enhanced. Two months after the celebrations, the White Paper named the College as one of 28 on a provisional list of Polytechnics, and Mr Crosland was to include it in his confirmed list of 29, which he announced on 5 April 1967.[19]

By then, about half of the new buildings planned in 1954 had been completed. The foundations of the first two - to be known, as long as they lasted, as the 'tower blocks' - were laid in 1957. There was some accommodation relief in the next session, when the Technical Teachers' Training College moved out to Halifax Road; and by September 1959 the Catering and Domestic Science Department occupied its new building and the Textiles and Engineering Departments their towers. But these were not net gains: buildings on the west side of Queen Street South had had to be demolished,[20] and such expedients resorted to as housing Music in a former YWCA building, a Sunday School and a warehouse whilst its block was being built.[21] It was painfully clear that a new site was needed for the Ramsden College, which still occupied part of the Old Building. Eventually, one was found, the former Royal Infirmary building, but it was not to be available until September 1968. The oldest building on the now-named Queensgate - St Paul's Church - was acquired for the College at this time. It was dedicated as a College Chapel by Dr Coggan, Archbishop of York, during an ecumenical 'College Mission' week, in March 1964.[22] In July 1965 the government curtailed the College's building programme, but by September 1966 the Music block was occupied - though already described as 'too

34. Dr. Donald Coggan, Archbishop of York

---

* Simultaneously, and relatedly, the Chairman of Governors - who was also Chairman of the Education Committee - ex-Alderman John L Dawson, resigned, after being defeated in the local-government elections of May 1964. He had been a Councillor since 1927, a Governor since 1934, and was Chairman of Governors for an unbroken period of 26 years, longer than any predecessor. A man of outstanding ability and force of character, he had exerted a decisive influence on educational policy in Huddersfield in the post-war generation.

small for present needs' - and plans for a 'Great Hall and Communal Block' were well advanced. The first College computer, a '4120 Central Processor', was installed, in an air-conditioned room, in June 1967.[23] The Library moved, with Humanities, Architecture (then part of the School of Art) and Mathematics, into 'Z Block' in the autumn of 1968, when also the 'Catering Annex' was occupied. In the Library's first year in Z Block, borrowings increased by 64 per cent and use of the Library 'for study and reference' was 'at least doubled'. In 1969-70, the Sports Hall complex and the Great Hall/Administration building came into use.[24] The inheritance of the Mechanics' Institution had by now descended on two colleges, on separate sites, though not yet wholly separated: Huddersfield Polytechnic, formally so designated in June 1970, and Ramsden Technical College, which in July 1971 was to resume the name Huddersfield Technical College.

When the 1966 White Paper had named Huddersfield as a proposed Polytechnic, the only degree-level courses the College taught were in Pure and Applied Chemistry and Electrical Engineering. In 1967, an ordinary degree in Chemistry was approved, and preparation was under way of honours submissions to the CNAA in Textile Marketing, Engineering Systems, European Studies in the Humanities Department, and Music, and of an ordinary degree in Catering.[25] Only the first was then successful, and teaching began for it in 1968. But both Chemistry and Electrical Engineering found difficulty in recruiting students, and a proposal for a degree in Engineering Design was rejected on the grounds of over-supply of degree-level places. The 'School of Music' gained the CNAA's conditional approval for an honours course, and the Humanities Department resumed teaching for the London external BA degree in 1969.[26] The academic evolution of the College overall is recorded in the changing composition of the student body. One-third of students were under 18 in 1962-3, 9.4 per cent were full-time and 94 per cent lived locally. The transfer of students to Ramsden Technical College and the increasing advanced-level work had measurable effects. In 1968-9, in a student total of 4,131 (additionally, there were 1,211 on short courses) 12.9 per cent were under 18; 25 per cent were full-time; and 77 per cent were resident locally.

35. Queen Street South c1960 looking south and showing (on the left) the Chemistry Building and beyond it, the original Technical College building of 1883

36. Students' Union

Dr Scott was a tireless promoter of collegiate life, among both students and staff. As there were annual staff walks and staff dinners, so there was a pattern of student activities through the academic calendar, which owed more to the Principal's paternalism than the students' initiative. The year began with a 'Student Day', called 'Freshers' Conference' from 1960, and opened by a religious service in the 'College Chapel'. Other regular features were charity-supporting activities - called 'Rag Week' from 1959-60 - which reached a high point in 1964-5, when £1,000 was raised; a number of student balls; and student-club activities. An annual 'Sports Day' of athletic events - for staff as well as students - was held in every year from 1949 to 1970. An early *victor ludorum* was D G (Derek) Ibbotson, then a Higher National Diploma student in engineering, who became an Olympic bronze medallist at 5,000 metres and world-record miler. In 1962 Ephraim S Kalungi broke Ibbotson's College record for 880 yards, with a time of 2 min. 8.5 secs. Ibbotson's contemporary was Ken Taylor, an Art student, who dominated a staff-student cricket match. The staff won a return game because Taylor was playing for Yorkshire. He also became the regular centre-half for Huddersfield Town, then a First Division side. The *Mock Turtle* student magazine was revived in 1948. Club activities expanded, despite meagre sports facilities, which prevented home fixtures. An 'International Student Society' was well supported by the College and in the town, and with increasing financial resources in the 1960s, there were much-improved Union facilities, and wider activities. These included political societies. They must have caused some concern in 1963-4. 'After considerable thought and discussion, it was agreed that clubs with a political bias be allowed to form so long as they were not affiliated with political parties outside the College and did not receive financial support from Student Union funds.' Delegates were sent to the 'NUS Council', and the College Union was a founder-member of the West Yorkshire Regional NUS. The Union lost its home on the demolition of the 'Princess Street Annexe' in 1968, and St Joseph's School, recently vacated, became the Union Building[*], as it turned out, for longer than anyone foresaw.[27]

---

[*] The St Joseph's Building was demolished in September 1995; on its site now stands a new Students' Union building.

37. Textiles Department. This building is located at the corner of Queen Street South (now Queensgate) and Princess Street, and opposite the 1883 building

Dr Scott addressed the academic staff at the beginning of every session, and usually told them that all depended on the quality of the staff. He listed staff publications in his annual reports religiously, and his solicitations sometimes elicited entries not-unfairly describable as light-weight. These lists continued to be dominated by the chemists, among whom the research impetus was sustained after Dr Hodgson was succeeded by Dr G R Ramage in 1948. But the output from other Departments testified to lively research activity across the academic spectrum. Another outstanding characteristic of Dr Scott was his knowledge of and attachment to the institution's history. When, in 1957, the foundations had been laid of buildings being financed under the 1956 White Paper, there was a last re-kindling of the old voluntary spirit, in the raising of £40,000 for 'purchasing equipment for the New Buildings'. Prominent in organising the appeal was Alderman H A Bennie Gray, who, at the age of 28, had come to Huddersfield from Scotland, in 1908, to manage the W C Holmes & Co engineering works. He had first joined the Governors' 'Extensions Sub-Committee' 40 years before, in, of all historic months, October 1917. Ten years after this 'New Buildings' appeal, in 1967, he was to be guest of honour, with Ms Holland, at a dinner held to celebrate 50 years of the Board of Studies. It also celebrated the foundation, also in 1917, of the Huddersfield Engineers' Training Association, of which he had been Chairman for nearly its whole existence.*[28] In the last annual report he wrote, in 1969, Dr Scott was 'pleased to note' 'the first degree awards in Electrical Engineering in this College under the CNAA', marking the end of 'a hard and long fight back from the days of the closure of the London External Degrees …' (in 1957). He regretted 'that two distinguished old students of engineering' (in the College) 'did not live to see the results'. Both had died that year. 'Edgar Lunn, aged 90, student from 1893 (West Riding Evening Scholarship), MIEE, rode to College on a Penny

---

* The University Library holds a valuable collection of books which Mr Bennie Gray bequeathed to it in 1958.

Farthing. For many years in charge of Huddersfield (Corporation) Electricity undertaking. Hon Vice-Chairman, Huddersfield Engineers' Training Association'. 'Arthur Sykes, aged 81, student from 1905, BSc 1914. World expert on gears. Hon Vice-Chairman, Huddersfield Engineers' Training Association ...'[29]

The College had played a part in another foundation in 1963 than that of Ramsden Technical College. In February, Huddersfield's Chief Education Officer, Harold Gray, had told the Board of Studies of the Authority's intention to set up a Day Training College for Teachers (in schools). He did this because it was intended that staff of the College would be 'responsible for the personal academic education of the students'.[30] The opening of Oastler College*, in September 1963, in premises rented from the Co-operative Retail Services, in New Street, fulfilled the hopes of Principals Rawson and Hudson, 60 years before, and revived an association with teacher training that the College had had for 20 years, and in a less-formal way for almost a century.[31] There was not as much common staffing across the colleges as Mr Gray had envisaged, but College of Technology staff taught academic subjects at Oastler, and when, in 1967, the Authority was invited to submit its scheme for a Polytechnic for approval by the Department of Education, it associated both colleges with the proposal.[32] On 17 July 1968 the Secretary of State formally announced that he would be 'prepared to designate the College of Technology, joined with Oastler College of Education, as a Polytechnic'. Staff representatives of both colleges worked with LEA officials to draw up an Instrument and Articles of Government, which the Department accepted in June 1969, and the nucleus of a Polytechnic Governing Body met in October. When an interim Polytechnic Academic Board was convened, in April 1970, Mr K J Durrands, whose career had mainly been in the nuclear engineering industry, and who had been appointed Director in November 1969, was present. The Polytechnic was instituted on 1 June 1970, and the designation ceremony was performed on 23 April 1971 by the new Secretary of State for Education and Science, Mrs Margaret Thatcher.[33]

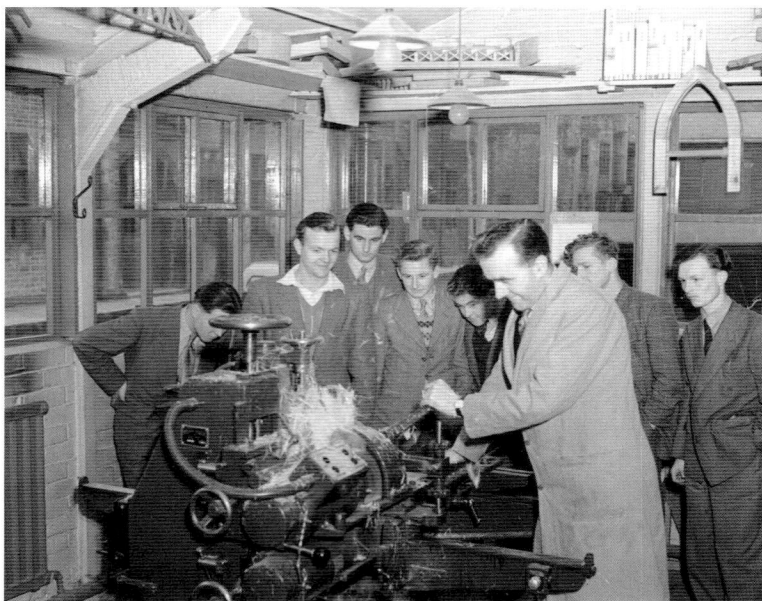

38. College Facility

---

* So named to honour Richard Oastler, the 'Tory Radical' campaigner against child labour in factories, and steward to the Thornhills - absentee owners of Fixby Hall and the 'Fixby Pastures' visited by the Mechanics' Institution's students and their lady friends in 1844 - but dismissed in 1838 for campaigning against the 'new Poor Law' of 1834.

Notes on Chapter 5

1. Lord President of the Council: *Scientific Manpower* (Barlow Report). HMSO, 1946; Michael Argles, *South Kensington to Robbins* (London, 1964).
2. Roy Lowe, *Education in the Post-War Years: A Social History* (London, 1988), pp.67, 159; Michael Argles, *South Kensington to Robbins* (London, 1964), p.101.
3. Principal's Report (PR) 1945-6, p.4; PR 1949-50, pp.6-7.
4. PR 1952-3, pp.3-4; 1947-8, p.10; 1948-9, p.14; 1949-50, pp.12-13; 1950-51, p.2.
5. PR 1948-9, pp.3-6; 1951-2, pp.2-4; 1949-50, p.4; 1956-7, p.2; 1966-7, pp.3-4.
6. PR 1945-6, pp.3-4; 1949-50, pp.1-3, 7; 1950-51, p.2.
7. PR 1952-3, p.3.
8. PR 1949-50, p.2; Proc Counc Finance S-C, 20.1.50, Min 456; *Huddersfield Daily Examiner* (HDE), 4 February 1954.
9. PR 1945-7, pp.3-4.
10. PR 1948-9, p.14; 1950-51, pp.2-3, 11.
11. *Technical Education*. Cmd. 9703. HMSO (1956); Ministry of Education, Circular 255; PR 1953-4, p.2; 1954-5, pp.2, 3.
12. PR 1953-4, p.2.
13. *Better Opportunities in Technical Education*, HMSO (1961); *A Plan for Polytechnics and Other Colleges*, Cmd. 3006, HMSO (1966); *Education: A Framework for Expansion*, Cmd. 5174, HMSO (1972); *Report of the Committee on Higher Education appointed by the Prime Minister*, Cmd. 2154, HMSO (1963-4, 6 volumes) (The Robbins Report).
14. Huddersfield College of Technology (HCOT), PR 1957-8, pp.2-3; 1959-60, p.4.
15. HCOT, PR 1961-2, p.3.
16. *Ibid*, p.2; HCBC Proc Counc, 1962.
17. HCOT PR 1963-4, pp.2-3. H M Dix, *Twenty Five Years On. A Short History of Huddersfield Technical College* (Huddersfield 1989).
18. HCOT PR 1964-5, p.3.
19. *A Plan for Polytechnics and Other Colleges*, HMSO (1966); Parliamentary Statement by the Secretary of State for Education & Science ... 5 April 1967.
20. HCOT PR 1958-9, p.2; 1967-8, pp.9, 19.
21. HCOT PR 1963-4, p.3; 1965-6, p.13.
22. HCOT PR 1963-4, ; H M Dix, *op cit*, pp.13-14.
23. HCOT PR 1965-6, p.4; 1966-7, pp.12, 16.
24. HCOT PR 1967-8, pp.2, 17-18, 19; 1968-9, p.14.
25. HCOT PR 1966-7, pp.6, 8, 11, 14, 15; 1967-8, pp.7-8, 9-10, 13, 16.
26. HCOT PR 1968-9, pp.10, 13, 14, 15.
27. HCOT PR *passim*.
28. HCOT PR 1956-7, pp.1, 8; 1957-8, p.3; 1967-8.
29. HCOT, PR 1968-9, pp.20, 10, 13.
30. HCOT, PR 1962-3, pp.3-4.
31. *Calendars* for 1903-4, p.272; 1904-5, pp.261-2; 1899-1900, p.183; *supra* pp.11, 12.
32. HCOT, PR 1966-7, p.2; Proc Counc, Governors of College of Technology and Ramsden Technical College, 22 November 1966 (Min. 296); 18 April 1967 (Min. 553); *HDE*, 24 October 1967; HCOT, PR 1968-9, p.4.
33. *HDE*, 23 April 1971.

PART II

The Polytechnic of Huddersfield, 1970-1992

CHAPTER 6

VI. Queen Street South Building

CHAPTER 6

THE ESTABLISHMENT OF THE POLYTECHNIC AND THE MERGER WITH HOLLY BANK, 1970-74

(a) The Establishment of the Polytechnic, 1970-72

On the day of the Polytechnic's official inception, 1 June 1970, Mr Durrands made an oral report to 'the Governing Council'. Two years later he submitted a 'Biennial Report … on the progress of the Polytechnic between 1 June 1970 and 31 May 1972', and presented the two reports printed in parallel.[1] He now envisaged polytechnics receiving their own charters 'by 1975 or 1980', and being 'funded more directly by Central Government'. This seemed to point to university status as an ambition, with polytechnics 'following the path set by the old CATs', but Mr Durrands was emphatic that it was 'to be hoped that this does not happen', and he was grateful for 'the strong support we have received from our Local Authority'.[2] The Department of Education and Science (DES) had estimated that in 10 years' time the 43 universities in the United Kingdom would have an average of 10,000 and the 30 polytechnics an average of 6,000 full-time-equivalent students each. Mr Durrands saw 4,500 as a 'full-time student' target for Huddersfield by 1981, with 2-3,000 part-time students.[3] In its first two years the Polytechnic's total student numbers, by head count, declined, mainly because of continuing transfers of lower-level work to the Ramsden college; the full-time-equivalent (FTE) number was constant, at about 2,200. Mr Durrands faced a problem of 'poolability'. Only courses which required A-Level entry qualified for funding from the national 'Advanced Further Education (AFE) Pool'; lower-level courses fell upon the local 'rates', and Huddersfield was a small Authority to bear such costs. The Director was anxious, however, to retain some such courses, especially in Textiles, 'to allow time for the build-up of high level academic work'. The level of work ranged from craft courses to doctoral research, and Mr Durrands committed himself to promoting courses of sub-degree level equally with undergraduate and higher-degree work and to 'keeping the traditions of our constituent colleges' by seeing that 'where possible our students should be equipped to do a job'. The 1972 report demonstrated how slow progress was to be at the higher levels: four new degree courses had been approved by the CNAA since 1970, and the College now taught nine CNAA-degree courses. The first of these, in Chemistry, had been approved in 1967. In March 1972, therefore, a panel appointed by the Council paid a first 'institutional quinquennial review' visit. Its benign report was issued in May, and the Governors 'expressed their satisfaction … at the progress made by the Polytechnic, as indicated by this report'.[4]

The Registrar of the College of Technology had resigned, and the Governors eventually created an administrative establishment of Chief Administrative Officer (CAO) and Deputy (DCAO), and a Registrar for academic and student affairs. By June 1971 Mr J T Blackwood and Mr K Sheard were in office as CAO and DCAO and Mr M E Bond as Registrar. In his report of June 1970 Mr Durrands had recommended to Governors that there should be three Assistant Directors (ADs), with defined areas of responsibility, who would also be Deans of Faculties. Miss Mary Dennell, who had been Vice-Principal and briefly Acting Principal of Oastler College, became Assistant Director for Personnel and

Welfare, and Dean of the Faculty of Education. The other two ADs were externally appointed. Mr Gerald Fowler, a classicist, who had been Minister for Higher Education in the Wilson administration and had lost his seat in the recent general election, was made Assistant Director for Academic Affairs and Dean of the Faculty of Arts, from September 1970. Dr Stewart Armstrong, a civil engineer, who came from Kingston Polytechnic, took up his post from January 1971, and was to be responsible for 'Resources' and to be Dean of the Engineering Faculty. Dr Eric Tittensor, Head of Chemistry, became Acting Dean of Sciences.

By the time the Director presented his 'biennial report', in June 1972, major changes were needed. Miss Dennell was shortly to retire, and Mr Fowler had already left. He had exercised a powerful formative influence on academic and organisational developments, and in the appointment of new staff; but his relations with the Director had so deteriorated that co-operation between them had virtually ceased. In view of the heavy building programme, and of a proposal, about to be made to the DES by the Huddersfield Authority, that the Polytechnic and the Huddersfield College of Education (Technical), at Holly Bank, on the Halifax Road, should merge, the Director decided that Assistant Directors should 'become ADs *per se*'. Dr Armstrong's title would be 'Planning', and a successor would be appointed to Miss Dennell. Three Deans of Faculty would be appointed from within, and the third Assistant Directorship, and the Deanship of Education, would be left vacant, awaiting developments from the merger proposal. There would thus be no AD for Academic Affairs, to succeed Mr Fowler.[5] New Departments were created in the Arts and Business subject areas, and one in the Engineering Faculty. The 14 Departments that the Polytechnic had inherited had now become 20 departments and four 'divisions', grouped into four Faculties.[6]

Mr Durrands was highly critical of the extent and condition of the Polytechnic's buildings. One of his earliest initiatives had been the appointment of consultant architects

39. Central Services Building and Tower

40. Polytechnic entrance. The Textile Department Tower is on the left and Z Block is on the right

to advise on building development. Dr Lewis Womersley, of the partnership Wilson and Womersley, drew up a plan, and the first instalment of what would become the Central Services Building (CSB) received DES approval early in 1972. In his evaluation of the Polytechnic's capital equipment the new Director's special concern was the 'mainframe' computer: it was four years old, but he described it as 'completely out of date'. A facility of wider use was the library. The total number of books in 1970 was given as 62,500, and Library expenditure in 1970-71 was £22,600. In the next two years, sums of £70,000 and £80,000 were spent, and the book total rose to 94,500. Building-development plans provided for 4,500 students and included 1,000 Library study places.[7]

There were 320.5 full-time-equivalent (FTE) members of the academic staff on Designation Day, of whom 27 were about to be transferred to Ramsden Technical College. Mr Durrands then estimated that 75 new appointments were needed in the next academic year; in fact, 131 were made in the next two years. The Director also encouraged the appointment of consultants, suitably qualified and experienced academics, and sometimes practitioners, who were usually paid annual fees of £250 plus expenses. Six had been appointed by June 1972, and the number steadily increased through the 1970s.[8]

The Polytechnic's first Fellowships were conferred at its formal designation ceremony, on 23 April 1971, when also a Polytechnic coat of arms was unveiled.[9] Alderman Douglas Sisson, the first Chairman of the Polytechnic's Governing Council, was by now described as 'President', reviving a title that went back to 1841, but had not been used since the municipalisation of the College in 1903. Mr Durrands was particular about titles. He concluded his 1972 report by explaining that he took 'great exception' to 'the use lately' of the word 'Directorate', 'as I and senior colleagues ... see ourselves more in the role of servants to the Institution'. It was 'more in keeping with this role ... to change my title to that of Rector', which '... is in line with that used by the Heads of similar institutions in the EEC countries'.

(b) The Merger with Holly Bank and Departments in Flux, 1972-74

In July 1971 Huddersfield's Chief Education Officer had told the Governors of both

41. Mrs Margaret Thatcher, Alderman Douglas Sissons and Mr Kenneth J Durrands at the Polytechnic's designation ceremony, 23 April 1971

42. Mrs Margaret Thatcher at the designation ceremony, 23 April 1971

institutions that the LEA had 'decided to initiate discussions on the proposition that the Huddersfield College of Education (Technical) should be integrated with the Polytechnic'. Mr Gray had written to the DES to announce this intention and to explain the reasons behind it. Contrary to its view in 1967, the Authority now considered it appropriate for a college which trained technical teachers 'to increase and intensify its ties with a practical, technological institution such as a Polytechnic'. The DES supported the proposal, and by April 1972 both Governing Bodies had approved it in principle.[10] Academic staff, particularly in the Holly Bank college, received it with suspicion and even hostility. After hard bargaining, a joint 'Statement of Intent' was agreed, in December. The LEA was asked to seek acceptance of it by the DES 'prior to submission of a formal proposal for merger'. Two of its clauses dealt with 'educational purposes'; seven with 'safeguards and conditions' for staff. One provided for retention of the College's name 'within the Polytechnic'; another for staffing at Holly Bank to be separately calculated, because 'high quality' and 'appropriate experience' were needed there. The Authority submitted this statement in January 1973.[11] Six months later the College asked the Authority to reconsider the merger proposal 'in the light of developments ... since it was made', and to appoint a new Principal to the College from January 1974, to succeed the retiring Mr A MacLennan. Some Polytechnic staff, in a context of public-expenditure cuts, feared the consequences for their own career prospects of assimilation into the Polytechnic of College staff whose current salary scale was lower than their own and whose salaries were therefore likely to be raised. They complained, too, about a large number of new appointments at the College, and about lobbying of the Huddersfield and the partly-formed Kirklees Education Committees by College staff.[12]

Despite the misgivings, both Governing Bodies approved the merger, and the Secretary of State authorised it on 7 February 1974. The new Kirklees Metropolitan Council (KMC) was recommended to make the 'amalgamation', from 1 September, and to accept the staffing proposals. The processes of merger were mentioned only incidentally at the Polytechnic's Academic Board meetings, but consequences were widespread and profound. Immediately, the salaries of the most senior staff - the 'Rectorate' - were raised, as the institution's size increased, and the post of Assistant Rector/Dean of Education was filled by Mr Frank Barr, who had been Vice-Principal of the College of Education. The Rectorate had already been expanded by the appointments of Mr T J Gaskell as Assistant Rector (Personnel and Welfare) and then Dr J Patterson, as an additional Assistant Rector, both from 1 January 1974. An alteration in academic organisation in March created two Faculties - Arts and Business - from the hitherto Faculty of Arts. This five-faculty system - Arts, Business, Education, Engineering and Sciences - was to continue until the creation of 'Schools' in April 1989.[13]

'School' is a term of varying meaning through the institution's history. It had been applied to Art since the 1840s, since 1966 to Music, and only in the Polytechnic era to Architecture, which till 1970 was within the School of Art. All of these ran into trouble in the early Polytechnic years. The long-term future of the 'School of Art and Design' - which in the 1960s had failed to gain approval for degree-equivalent work - was doubtful; but it was pointed to in the early 1970s. An attempt by the Department of Textile Industries to form a partnership with Bradford College of Art came unstuck; a result of this was that Art and Design staff would find a home mainly within Textiles.[14]

43. A view of the Central Services Building

Architecture was re-housed in January 1971 from its converted bus depot, a mile from the campus, to suitably-adapted space nearby, above the newly-built Market Hall. But that year's report on the Part-I examinations of the Royal Institute (RIBA) was so alarming that publication of results was postponed, and the Governors resolved that there could be no intake of new students in September. In the autumn term, amid crisis meetings, the Architecture students organised a sit-in and presented a set of demands. The Governors' solution was to agree to the formation of 'a broad-based Department headed by a Grade VI Head', who would also be an 'Associate Dean', and be supported by additional staff and two consultants. Such a senior appointment caused staff re-gradings elsewhere in the Polytechnic. These costly measures secured the School's future.[15]

Student militancy was not confined to Architecture. It became endemic in the 'School of Music'. In 1963, when the Ramsden college had been founded, Music was not, like other Departments, split: one Department provided Music teaching in both colleges, and its Head nominally supervised the LEA's schools music service. From September 1971 the 'School of Music' was divided for teaching purposes into a 'Senior School' in the Polytechnic and a 'Junior School' in the Technical College. Each School had a Head, but they were the only staff appointed to either institution: the rest were appointed to the Authority. In his June 1972 Report, Mr Durrands claimed that this oddly-named 'Combined School of Music' exacerbated his 'poolability' problem: the problem of having teaching which did not qualify for higher-education funding. This ill-conceived scheme, and the inherent expensiveness - in staffing, equipment and space-requirements

- of teaching music, combined to turn the clash of personalities involved into a running battle which lasted till 1977. The Music Department had occupied a new building in 1966; but it was too small, and outlier buildings were still used. In 1972 the building of a 'teaching block' adjacent to the Music building was authorised. The music staff - and, militantly, the music students - claimed it should be for them, but it was designated an 'Arts Study Block': for use generally by the Arts Faculty. In April 1973 the Governors were petitioned by all the music staff and students to accept a management solution that would have made the School semi-independent. The Rector pointed out the anomaly of a management scheme which made only the Head of Department a member of the Polytechnic's staff and thus answerable to the Academic Board for the Polytechnic's courses. At the end of 1974, when the Department's BA course was due for its quinquennial re-approval by the CNAA, student demand triumphantly secured exclusive use of the 'Arts Study Block' to Music, but the 'administration of the Huddersfield School of Music' was unchanged and still unsatisfactory. By that time the accommodation problem was general in the Polytechnic, and made more acute because the 'Catering and Administration building' had been declared structurally unsound, and was about to be demolished.[16]

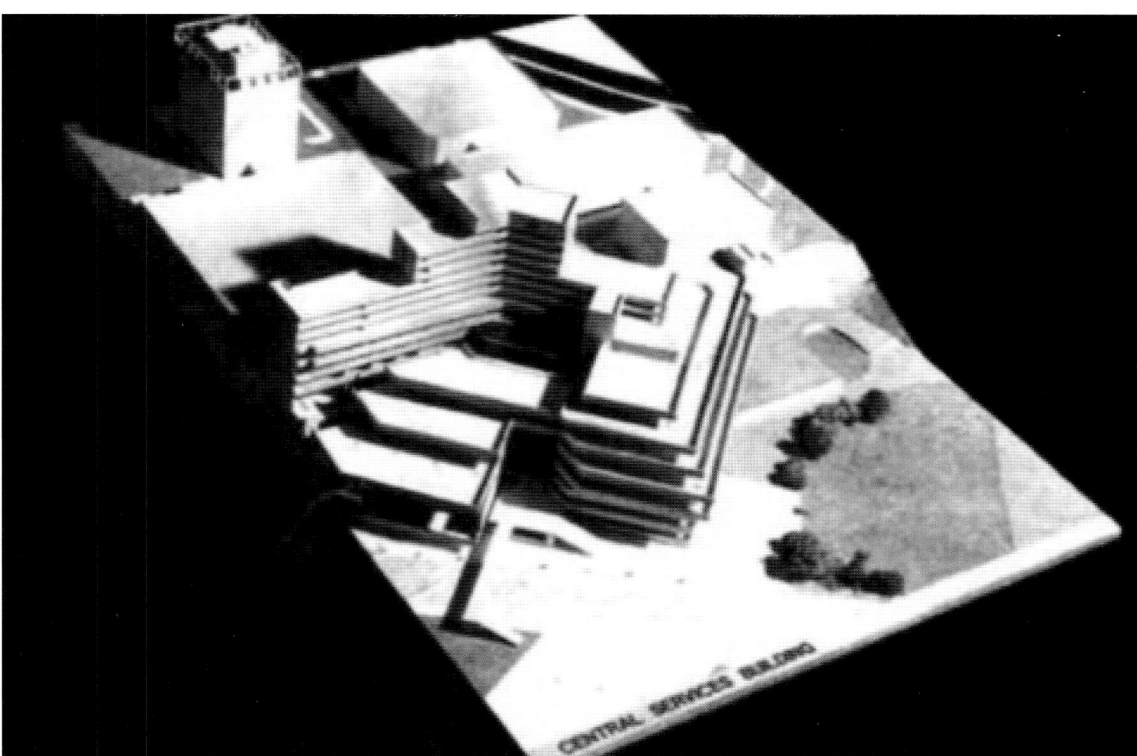

44. Architect's model of the Central Services Building

Notes on Chapter 6

1. Huddersfield Polytechnic. Governors' Minutes (Govs mins) 72/63; 'The Polytechnic, Huddersfield. Director's Report (DR) to the Governing Council, June 1970 and June 1972'.
2. DR 1970 and 1972, pp.1-6.
3. In 1981-2 there were to be 4,300 full-time and sandwich students, and 1,700 part-time students.
4. DR pp.9-17; letter, 18 May 1972, and report of visit on 15 March 1972. Govs min 72/85; Academic Board min (Ac Bd) 71/363.
5. Letter of Chief Education Officer, HCBC, 20 July 1971; DR June 1972, pp.22-6.
6. HCBC mins 167c: FE S-C; DR 1970, 1972, p.44; Ac Bd 71/225; DR pp.24, 26-30.
7. DR, 1972, pp.31-5; HCBC min. 337(b); DR pp.36-7, 52.
8. DR pp.38-40.
9. Ac Bd mins, 26 March 1971.
10. Govs min 38, 16 August 1971; HCBC min 475, FE S-C, 13 April 1972.
11. HCBC min 373: Educ Comm, 22 December 1972; Ac Bd, 72/144, 7 December 1972; 72/146, 14 December 1972; Govs min 72/100, 15 December 1972.
12. HCBC min 94, 12 July 1973; Govs mins 73/76, 73/112, 74/21; HCBC min 256, 15 November 1973; Ac Bd 73/25, 26 November 1973.
13. HCBC mins 381, 389, 14 February 1974; Ac Bd 74/35; HCBC mins 427, 428, 14 March 1974; 453, 25 March 1974; Kirklees Metropolitan Council (KMC) mins, 25 October 1973, 13 December 1973, 18 April 1974; Mins of Govs S-C, 5 July 1974; 27 September 1974, 15 October 1974, 15 November 1974; Govs mins G/74/118, G/75/3, G/73/91; HCBC min 30, FE S-C, 13 December 1973; Govs mins G/74/11; KMC mins, April-October 1974, min 20, 14 May 1974.
14. HCOT PR, 1962-3, p.12; DR 1970 and 1972, p.42; Govs min 70-71/92; Ac Bd 71/199, 71/357, 73/110, 74/59.
15. Ac Bd 71/202; DR 1970 and 1972, 42; Govs min 70-71/63; HCOT PR, 1968-9, p.6; Ac Bd 71/370, 371; 71/374; 71/375B; Govs min 65, 26 October 1971; DR 1972, p.40; Govs min 66-68, 26 October 1971; Ac Bd 73/104; Govs min 73/44, 2 April 1973.
16. Govs min 73/68; Ac Bd 73/44, 73/101; 74/29; 74/54; 74/83; 74/102; 'A Critical Review of Music. Report to the Rector for the information of Academic Board', 30 October 1974; Ac Bd 74/147; Govs min 73/111; HCBC min 191, 24 September 1973; Govs min 73/110; 73/144; 74/138; 75/1; 75/36; Ac Bd 74/128.

CHAPTER 7

VII. Central Services Building

CHAPTER 7

ADJUSTING TO KIRKLEES, AND THE CRISIS OF 1979-81, (1974-1981)

(a) Adjusting to Kirklees, 1974-79

The Polytechnic's relations with Kirklees Metropolitan Council (KMC) were never smooth. Alderman Sisson, a Conservative, retired as President when the Local Government Act came into effect on 1 April 1974. There was a Labour majority on Kirklees Council, and hence a Labour Chairman of the Education Committee and the Polytechnic Governing Body. It was to be so for 11 of the 15 years until the Polytechnic became a Higher Education Corporation, in 1989. The Rector's relations with his Governors and Education Authority changed markedly after re-organisation. Already in January 1974 the Polytechnic's revenue estimates for 1974-5 were 'referred back' by the nascent KMC's Education Committee, a setback he had never experienced.[1] Through the financial year 1974-5, Councillor Mrs Jessie Smith, Chairman of the Education Committee, was elected *ad hoc* to chair each Governors' meeting; then from April 1975, now gazetted CBE, she was Chairman.* Conditioning the frigid relations of the Rector with the Governors and the Authority was a national context in which the Labour government faced a financial crisis. By autumn 1975, inflation was running at 26 per cent per annum, and from January there had been pressure on the Polytechnic, from the National Pooling Committee and the LEA, to function more economically. While the Academic Board was devising a required five-year plan, and Mr Gaskell's calculations were revealing over-generous academic-staff/student ratios (SSRs), the Rector complained about 'a serious shortage of academic services staff', which made it difficult 'to ensure the proper handling of public money'.[2] In October 1975 Kirklees imposed a 'nil-growth budget' for the financial year 1976-7, proposing a £392,000 cut in the Polytechnic's estimates. The Rector deplored the 'serious implications for growth' and for adequate staffing of the new Central Services Building. The budget for 1976-7 was not agreed till November 1976,[3] when the Rector suddenly recommended its acceptance by Academic Board.

He did so partly because a new 'Relationship Document', negotiated between him and the Kirklees Chief Executive, had come into force. The Labour-controlled Education Committee had been suspicious of this,[4] but the new Conservative Chairman, Councillor Mrs Jane Carter, secured its endorsement in October 1976. It was a triumph for the Rector: it granted a degree of financial autonomy, and discretion about staffing.[5] But in doing so it contravened the Instrument of Government, and this incensed some Governors, including some Staff Governors. They organised the censuring of the Chairman and the Rector for this infringement of the rules. The Rector could carry Academic Board with him; at Governors' meetings, though he had the Chairman's support, there was an opposition group. Undeterred by the reprimand, however, in December 1976 he persuaded the Board to invite the Director of the Polytechnic of Central London (PCL), Dr Colin Adamson, to address members on how to make the Polytechnic a 'company limited by guarantee', and thus independent of the LEA. But PCL was not a model for Huddersfield: as the former Regent Street Polytechnic, uniquely

---

* Mrs Smith repudiated the title 'President', but was happy to be called 'Chairman'.

45. Ramsden Building in the 1970s

among the polytechnics, it had never been answerable to an LEA.[6]

The Instrument of Government was the document that laid down the composition and powers of the Governing Body. Since the 1974 merger it had been under revision. In February 1977 the dissentient group of Governors - four Labour Councillors and three staff members - called a special meeting to discuss '…amendments carried by the (Conservative-controlled) Education Committee …' to the revised Instrument proposed by the Governors. These amendments would increase the size and alter the balance of the Governing Body. The dissentients persuaded a majority of Governors that Kirklees Council should be asked to reject its Education Committee's amendments, and that if it refused, the Governors' version, as well as the Council's, should be sent to the DES. Both were sent, and the Council was subsequently required 'to submit a revised draft … closer to that proposed by the Governors'.[7] The Rector was thus rebuffed. But he prevailed in another running battle, which he had waged for three years, against both the DES's officials and HM Inspectors. Arguing that the future of polytechnics depended on the quality of their facilities, he secured for Huddersfield a new computer of a capacity admittedly beyond its then needs, and correspondingly expensive. The Rector was congratulated when it was installed in May 1978.[8]

Other negotiations with the DES were about matters vital to the Faculty of Education. In March 1976 the Department initiated regional discussion about 'rationalisation' of initial training of school teachers to control the over-supply. Early in 1977 it proposed 'amalgamation' of such provision in the Polytechnic and Bretton Hall College, near Wakefield. All parties involved were opposed, and relieved when the threat was removed, in July. But in November, the Further Education (technical-teacher) departments of the

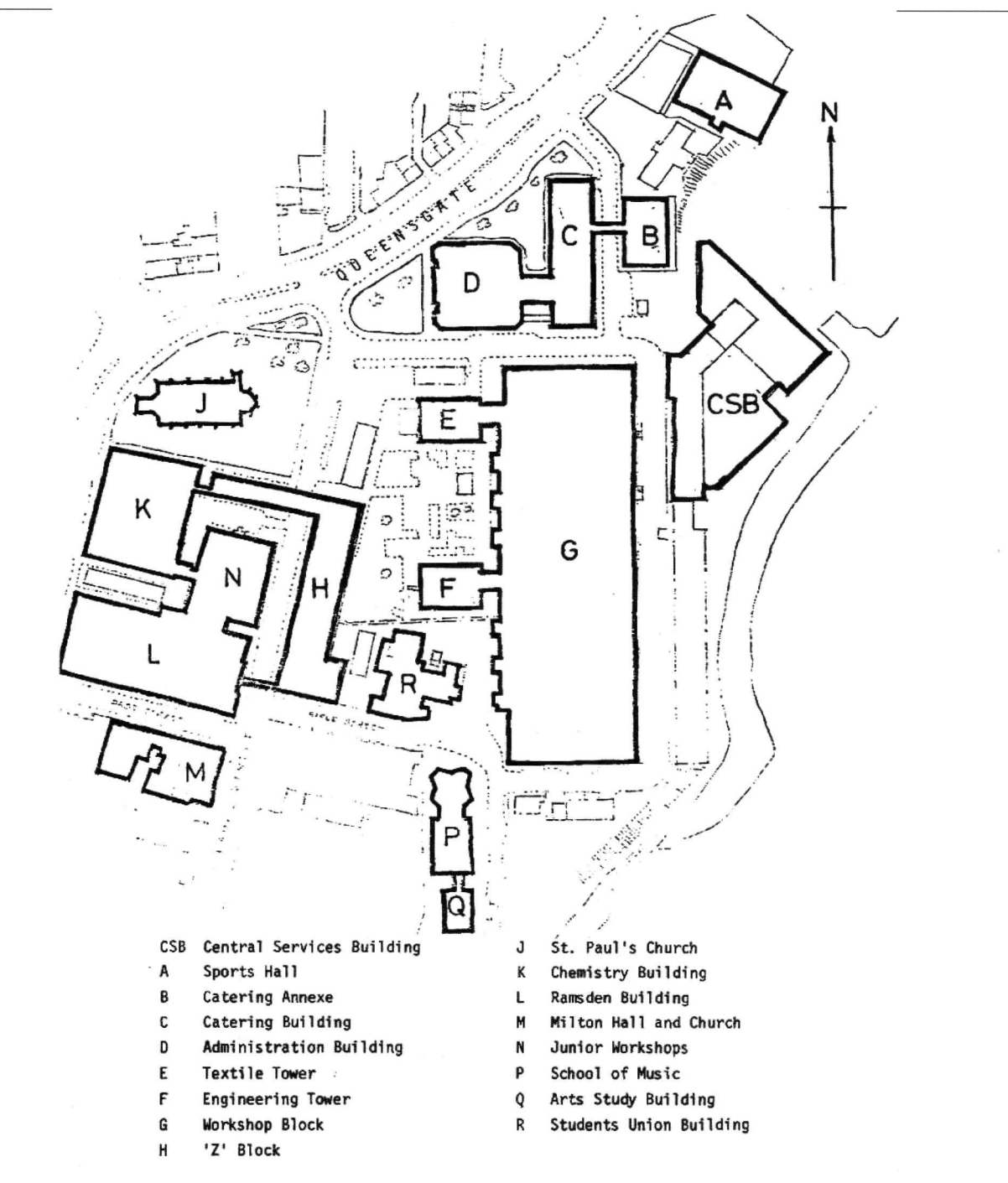

CSB	Central Services Building	J	St. Paul's Church
A	Sports Hall	K	Chemistry Building
B	Catering Annexe	L	Ramsden Building
C	Catering Building	M	Milton Hall and Church
D	Administration Building	N	Junior Workshops
E	Textile Tower	P	School of Music
F	Engineering Tower	Q	Arts Study Building
G	Workshop Block	R	Students Union Building
H	'Z' Block		

46. Map of the Polytechnic campus in 1975

Faculty were reported to be in danger of losing 30 posts because of the government's decision to restrict entry of overseas students into Britain from 1978-9. The Faculty was urged to develop new courses and a research programme, and a start was made with a 'Graduate Certificate in Education' course, though Academic Board was displeased that application for approval of it was made to Leeds University, and not to the CNAA.[9]

The Department most experienced in displeasing Academic Board was Music. It had three strings to its bow - staffing and resources, relations with the CNAA, and the organisation of the 'School of Music' - and they were intertwined. Staff appointments were not made because though, in 1975, the CNAA had re-approved its degree courses,

47. Queensgate Studios, Market Hall – a town centre location for part of the School of Art in the 1970s

it was inefficiently administered, partly because the organisation was wrong. Continually, the students demanded more staff and resources. A letter from the CNAA 'appeared to suggest that there could be no intake ... in September (1976)', but it was then 're-interpreted' by the Council. The same alarm was rung in 1977. What made a settlement possible was the Head of Department's retirement. But it was not till April 1978 that a formula was produced, by Dr Armstrong, supported by Mrs Carter, that became 'the seeds of an agreement'. Staff were to be allocated to separate departments, in the Polytechnic and the Technical College, and a joint committee of Governors was to meet as necessary. It seemed the obvious solution.[10]

The 'Relationship Document' agreed with Kirklees in 1976 had given the Polytechnic greater freedom in spending its financial allocations, but not unlimited resources. Mr Gaskell's 'optimistic' estimates for 1977-8 were trimmed, and those for 1978-9 'reduced substantially', despite the Rector's protests. Ominously, in October 1978, the Rector told Academic Board that there were 'differences between the Polytechnic and the Kirklees Director of Finance over the Relationship Document'. The Polytechnic's negotiator was now Mr P H Fielden. Appointed as 'Principal Staff Officer', in 1977, he became 'Manager' and, in March 1979, 'Director of Academic Support Services' (DASS), with an intended status of 'Deputy Director for Administration and Finance'. Changes among the senior staff had been made possible because of the early retirement of Dr Armstrong. As Deputy Rector, from 1974, he became unhappy with some developments, and gradually moved to the position where, in April 1978, he announced that he would retire in August. The Governors accepted the Rector's re-organisation plan of 'three Pro Rectors, in line with practice at the Universities'. The Rector's intentions for Mr Fielden were apparent; but there were to be difficulties in trying to fulfil them.[11]

48. Co-operative Building – a temporary location for academic activity

(b) Mounting Troubles and the Crisis of 1979-81

A second 'quinquennial institutional review' visit to the Polytechnic by the CNAA had been made on 3-4 March 1977. Despite Academic Board's enquiries, no report of this was produced till January 1979, and before the Board could discuss it, it had been leaked to the *Huddersfield Daily Examiner*, which gave front-page publicity to the criticisms it contained. In fact, the report was generally favourable, particularly to the Rector, who was credited with 'positive and vigorous leadership'. But the exceptional delay was unexplained, and, also strangely, a response was not made to the CNAA till late-November 1979. By then, the Polytechnic was again front-page news. It was reported that Kirklees Council had discussed 'alleged mis-application by the Polytechnic of the Burnham scale of salaries …' Through the first half of December, five reports appeared in the *Examiner* about proposals for Kirklees to take disciplinary action.[12]

Confrontation had built up over a year. In November 1978 Kirklees had appointed external auditors to the Polytechnic, on the advice of its Directorate of Finance, which was carrying out an 'internal audit'. In February 1979 the Rector and Mr Fielden presented a 'consultative document' on '… the control and management of the Polytechnic's finances …' to the Academic Board, and invited it '… to make resolutions'. The Board obliged. It called on Governors to challenge the Authority's right to send in auditors, and demanded revision of the Polytechnic's Articles of Government and of the Kirklees/Polytechnic 'Relations Document' agreed in 1976. It was 'strongly of the view that the Polytechnic should become a company limited by guarantee' (like the Polytechnic of Central London). A further area of conflict was opened when Pro Rector Barr and Mr Fielden persuaded the Board to 'strongly re-affirm its decision to run the

49. Queen Street Annexe – a temporary location for part of the School of Music and the Department of Marketing and Accounting

Shiraz Course',* and in July Mr Fielden, now 'DASS', was asked to meet DES officials urgently 'to seek necessary changes to facilitate such courses'.[13]

The Governors did not discuss the 'Shiraz' short-courses problem until November 1979, when they considered two audit reports, the District Auditor's report to Kirklees Council and the report of the Council's Director of Finance. The Rector was absent, and Mr Barr defended the Shiraz and 'other short courses', which, he conceded, would increase 'the rate fund contribution' by 'about £350,000' that year. It was now that the *Huddersfield Examiner* published its sequence of sensational reports. They revealed a 'controversial report', 'being kept secret by Kirklees Council', which followed 'a nine-month audit of the Polytechnic', and which accused it 'of being inefficient in its financial arrangements'; and it reported the Labour leader, Councillor Lawrence Conlon, as having called upon 'the Tories' 'to quit as the Kirklees ruling party'. On 11 December a Council committee, in secret session, recommended 'disciplinary action' against the Polytechnic for the 'alleged maladministration', and take-over of the Polytechnic by Kirklees chief officers.[14] A hastily-convened Academic Board recorded 'its complete confidence … in the leadership of the Rector'. It 'unanimously' opposed 'the reported suggestion of a take-over by the Local Authority, or interference by them … in the … management of the Polytechnic'; invited the Secretary of State 'to institute a public enquiry into the relationship between' Kirklees Council and the Polytechnic; and deplored the Authority's use of 'the public news media' to make known its 'intentions'.

---

* Shiraz is the centre of the oil region of Iran. The Polytechnic's Centre for Overseas Education, located at Holly Bank, had arranged for Iranian students to come to Huddersfield on short courses. The Polytechnic received 'full-cost' fees for them, but these were paid into a Polytechnic account, and not to Kirklees; and because of the way the courses were run, they reduced the Polytechnic's 'poolability' percentage. The charges transferred from the 'AFE pool' to local rates far exceeded the income generated from the fees.

50. Music Department, gathered together in Huddersfield Town Hall

The Governing Body was as supportive. It appointed five Governors – the Chairman (Mrs Carter), the Rector, an 'industrialist' (Mr G C F Harding), a trade unionist (Mr R C Cross) and an academic (Professor G Black, of UMIST) – to 'receive a copy of the audit report' and any other information about 'alleged' 'maladministration of the Polytechnic's financial and other affairs', 'with powers to take appropriate action and report back ...'; it authorised the Rector 'to appoint legal advisers to advise and act for the Polytechnic'; and empowered the Chairman, Rector and DASS, 'with legal advice', to 'take such actions as their duty requires to protect the proper interests of the Polytechnic ...'[15]

In January 1980 the Rector reported to Governors and Academic Board on developments relating to revenue estimates for 1980-81 and to the 'internal audit report'. He persuaded the Governors to propose to the DES that the Polytechnic should be 'centrally funded', and to Kirklees that it should join with them in asking for a public enquiry; and he assured the Board that he would press for copies of the audit report to be made available in the Polytechnic. Majorities at the Governors' meeting accepted his appointment of 'Broomheads and Neals', of Sheffield, as legal advisers, and supported his deploring of what he claimed was a 'shortfall' of over £1.5m in the Polytechnic's budget proposed by Kirklees for 1980-81. While the Rector was in hospital, in March, the Governors refused to endorse the appointment by 'the Five Governors' of accountants Peat, Marwick, Mitchell & Co, 'to carry out a review of the internal systems of the Polytechnic'.[16] Mr Durrands had returned by mid-April, when the actions of the Five Governors were supported 'unconditionally' by the Academic Board, but were challenged at a meeting of

51. Trinity Hall – student accommodation

Governors specially convened by Labour Councillor members under the 1944 Education Act. It was attended by HMI A Arnison, the 'College Inspector'; the Kirklees Chief Executive and the Director of Educational Services; and Mr C D Trippett of Broomheads and Neals. A motion, to support 'the continuation of outside legal and financial advice', and an amendment to it – moved by Labour Councillors Mernagh and Mason – condemning a 'court action commenced by the Chairman and four Governors against Kirklees MC' and 'to terminate the purported employment of Broomheads and Neals', were proposed and seconded. The Kirklees officers and Mr Arnison counselled moderation and reconciliation, but the amendment was put. It was defeated, and the Chairman, Mrs Carter, 'to give the Local Authority an opportunity to show by some clear gesture of goodwill that they wish to co-operate on the resolution of difficulties arising from actions of Kirklees MC', adjourned the meeting, leaving 'the proposed resolution' (supporting 'the Five Governors' and thus the Rector) 'on the table'. When this 'Special Meeting' was re-convened, it resolved that 'the Local Authority be invited' to make a 'joint approach to the DES to appoint a person of high standing to arbitrate' ... between the Authority and the Polytechnic. This was the origin of the ill-fated 'Layfield enquiry'. 'The proposed resolution' remained 'on the table'.[17]

In meetings in May and into June, the Rectorate told Governors and Academic Board, with Mr Arnison present on two occasions, that the Polytechnic's 'budget allocation of £12,488,000 ... represents a shortage of £1.6m', that 'at least £800,000' needed to be added to 'the revenue allocation' to allow the Polytechnic to fulfil 'its basic function', and that there would be a 'deficit of £270,000 on salaries and wages' unless 'budget headings from which sums (could) be transferred' were identified. The Board agreed that the Rector should inform the CNAA that 'in the Board's judgement', 'current ... funds are likely to be completely exhausted by January 1981 ...' if courses were to be taught

52. Trinity Hall – student accommodation

'at the minimum acceptable academic level'.[18]

But after the May elections of 1980 both Kirklees Council and the Governing Body had Labour majorities. Mrs Carter, though still Councillor, and a member of the Education Committee, was no longer a Governor, and Councillor John Mernagh became Chairman of both the Committee and Governors. A 'scheme' for the running of the Polytechnic, reportedly devised by the Kirklees Chief Executive and the Rector, was 'received' by the Governors. Kirklees Council had approved it, and Mr Dixon was 'in touch' with the DES about it. The Governors set up an 'enquiry', to which the Rector was to submit 'a detailed Revenue Budget of income and expenditure'. Between two meetings in July the atmosphere at Academic Board changed dramatically, a change brought about by radical measures decided upon by the Governors in the interval. In the first meeting the Board still vigorously supported the Rector in his reporting to the CNAA the Polytechnic's difficulties in teaching its courses, and in warning the Governors that 'its academic credibility is being questioned'. Then, on 22 July, after a day-long scrutiny of reports from Polytechnic and Council Officers, the Governors imposed drastic economies, including a 'moratorium' on staff appointments, and ordered the officers 'to prepare budget alternatives within the approved allocation'. Told of this the next day, 'the Board recognised that national and local pressures to increase student/staff ratios (SSRs) could not be ignored, (and) accepted that this process would inevitably entail some loss of jobs'. The Rector was asked to inform the DES and the CNAA of these resolutions.[19]

Advised by Kirklees officers, the Governors now imposed a reform programme. There was to be reduced capital expenditure in 1980-81 and transfer of the money saved to other budget headings; and early-retirement terms were to be offered to interested staff. The Rector was to supply information about staff teaching hours and the SSRs on all courses, and organisation at Head of Department level and above was to be reviewed. An

53. Trinity Hall – student accommodation

Academic Plan to achieve, by summer 1982, the government-set SSR norm of 10:1* was to be submitted to Governors by November 1980. The Authority was to be asked to finance early-retirement and redundancy costs. Councillors Mernagh, Conlon and Mason represented the Governors at a meeting, 'urgently requested' by the CNAA, on 19 August, and it was then public knowledge that the Secretary of State had appointed Sir Frank Layfield, QC, 'to find a solution to the controversial audit dispute'.[20]

Following the Kirklees Finance Director's guidance, the Governors transferred £239,000 from revenue and £142,000 from capital expenditure to purchase equipment, and the Rector informed Academic Board that '£481,000 … could be made available against the shortfall …' How the figures were reconciled is not recorded. With that comfort, the Rector slipped out of an Academic Board meeting and arranged another emergency visit by CNAA officers, for the next day, 28 August. At this meeting, the officers expressed 'grave concern' about whether 'the environment of the Polytechnic' could maintain satisfactory standards for the CNAA's awards. They asked why, in view of earlier statements about the calamitous effects of the budget 'shortfall', a sum of £481,000, even 'provided it materialised', could now be seen as enough to maintain standards. The answer given was that it could 'with difficulty and sacrifice', and only 'in the current financial year', and that 'a considerable improvement' next year would be 'essential'.[21] In October, the CNAA's Chief Officer, Dr Edwin Kerr, asked to be informed about developments. When he received the Rector's reply, he wrote to say that members of the Council's Committee for Institutions - its most influential committee - would visit the Polytechnic in January 1981. This pleased Mr Durrands, but was considered unwarranted interference by Councillor Mernagh, 'in view of the relatively recent meetings and the

---

*   The Polytechnic's ratio at the time was 7.3:1.

54. Bankfield House - student accommodation

assurances then given ...' He wanted the DES, which 'had a major responsibility for the ... financial situation facing the Polytechnic', to be told about 'the CNAA involvement' in its affairs. Meanwhile, the tightening-up went on. The Governors gave the Rector a deadline of 1 June 1981 to produce the 'Review of Organisation' they had asked for on 11 August, and drastic cost-saving measures were imposed. A report on the 54 research posts and the funding of the 86 registered research-degree candidates was asked for, and a comparison with how other polytechnics financed research. Most of the Polytechnic's 'Site Services' staff were transferred to Kirklees Technical Services, and the catering services were scrutinised.[22]

Councillor Mernagh wanted 'a joint approach to the CNAA to be worked out with the Academic Board', but developments in the weeks that preceded the January visit did not make for co-operation. Board members were perturbed 'over the great danger to the institution if restrictions were to be placed on recruitment to courses', which was a real possibility if the CNAA's visiting party was not satisfied. When Mr Gaskell presented budget proposals for 1981-2 the KMC Finance Director advised Governors that the proposals 'failed to tackle the problems ...': the Polytechnic needed 'to reduce its Academic staff to below 500 FTE (from over 600) and Non-Academics to below 300' by September. The Academic Board had to consider urgently ''the implications of moving to a student/staff ratio of 9.2:1 in 1981-2 and 10:1 in 1982-3'. The Rector warned darkly about the need to re-structure courses '... particularly in view of the decline in students entering Higher Education'.* He suffered a rebuff when the Governors refused his request that Mr Fielden should be associated with the three Pro Rectors in the 'corporate management of the Polytechnic' during his own forthcoming visit to Brazil - on behalf of a UN Development Programme - which would take place after the CNAA visit. Then,

---

* Despite the unwelcome publicity, Huddersfield's total number had increased by 65, to 4,632 FTE, in 1980-81.

56. Bay Hall – student accommodation

of its academic work', and noted that the CNAA's letter 'passes no adverse judgement on the quality of its courses and teaching'. The letter had described Huddersfield Polytechnic as 'a major national institution of higher education ...' Issue of the statement was authorised by the Governors, and the Chairman agreed to enter talks about 'distinctive roles'. Governors and Academic Board had come together, and the Board's next ordinary meeting, on 20 March, was the one occasion in this crisis when the Board clearly took its own line. 'Ordinary business' was suspended, and the Rector was asked to 'give his interpretation' of the letter, 'drawing on clarifications he had had from the CNAA'. The Board was impatient for action, and a motion was proposed and seconded to draw the Secretary of State's attention to Dr Kerr's letter and to ask for his intervention. It was resolved that the motion 'be not put but it lie on the table'. The Board secondly resolved 'that the report of Sir Frank Layfield be made available at the earliest opportunity'; and thirdly, 'to accept that there is substance in the concerns expressed in the letter ... from the Chief Officer of the CNAA ..., and to urge the Governing Council that it take no action until ... the distinctive roles of and ... relationships among the Local Authority, Governing Council, Academic Board and Rector ...' had been defined. The meeting was 'adjourned sine die'.[24]

55. Bankfield House – student accommodation

at a Governor's meeting on 23 December 1980, came a much bigger setback for the Rector. After a complaint about Mr Fielden's having interfered with proceedings at a sub-committee meeting, the 'DASS' was barred from attending Governors' meetings until the allegation had been investigated. He left the Polytechnic immediately, and was not to return from sick leave until 1 October 1981. Strangely, however, the Rector's difficulties were to be greatly alleviated by the Chairman's next move. A 'Central Unit' was established 'for the purpose of achieving planned minimum reductions of 75 in the number of academic staff by September 1981'. To this 'Unit', with the Rector, were appointed Pro Rector Gaskell and Mr M N Drayton, a staff Governor, Kirklees Labour Councillor and prominent trade unionist. His presence was to make a difficult staff-reduction exercise acceptable.[23]

During 1981 the Rector's fortunes descended to their nadir and then recovered spectacularly. On 12 March the Governors received the CNAA's letter, dated 19 February, about the 22 January visit. Dr Kerr warned that 'unless the Polytechnic puts its own house in order and finds a solution to its longstanding financial wrangle with Kirklees, (the CNAA would) withdraw approval from its courses'. These requirements had to be met by 'the end of the current academic year'. The Governors invited the Academic Board's reactions, assuring it that they 'had every confidence' in its ability 'to deal with the academic issues raised'. In turn, the Board had 'every confidence' that the Governors would seek to 'establish ... distinctive roles' for themselves, the Authority, the

57. Warrenfield – student accommodation

further consideration of the motion now mentioned be deferred and that it lay (*sic*) on the table until 1st June 1981 at the latest'. The Governors then set up a working party 'to define distinctive roles and relationships' of LEA, Governors, Board and Rector 'within the provisions of the Articles of Government'. Questioned at the next Governors' meeting, on 28 April, the Rector 'confirmed … his intention to inform Academic Board of his statement and assurances' of 23 March. The Board met three times in May - though the Rector was absent from one meeting - and no announcement was made. Challenged again by Governors on 12 June, the Rector confirmed that 'it was still his intention to inform Academic Board of his statement and assurances'. That meeting 'considered the resolution ('the motion now mentioned') which had lain on the table since the meeting of 23 March 1981' and decided that it 'continue to lay on the table pending receipt of Sir Frank Layfield's report …' The Rector at last made a 'statement concerning his relationship with the Governing Body' to Academic Board on 3 July. He said that 'though as Rector and as a Governor he might not always agree with decisions properly made by the Governing Body, he willingly accepted that it was his duty as Rector to carry out the Governors' decisions as effectively as possible'. This announcement bore little relation to the 'statement and assurances' he had given to Governors on 23 March, but its

58. 22 Greenhead Road – student accommodation

quinquennial 'institutional review' which the CNAA had announced would take place in March 1982. This news also made urgent the need to approve and implement the Rector's proposals for the 'Academic Organisation of the Polytechnic', which included the creation of a 'School of Education', consisting of four departments, and of a Department of Humanities, which was a merging of four departments. On 10 July, bogged down in details, the Governors gave 'powers to act' on organisation, academic planning and appointments to a 'Review Group', and abandoned their enquiry into research funding. They approved the Rector's proposals for a new administrative structure, 'subject to … clarification of the position' of Mr Fielden - who was still on sick leave - following the internal appointment as 'Chief Administrative Officer' of Mr K Sheard. Among staff accepting redundancy or early-retirement terms, they noted, were six Heads of Departments.[26]

Mr Fielden's deposition was a bitter pill for the Rector, and little more palatable was the 'Review Group's' ruling that Pro Rector Dr Patterson 'be declared institutionally redundant' and 'that the Rector's proposal to transfer (him) to an Academic Department on a protected salary …' be accepted. The torment was added to when the Kirklees Chief Executive reported that he had sent a 'final draft of revised Articles of Government to the Rector some time ago', and that it must be submitted to Governors, since the Articles were essential to any settlement of the 'relationships' that had so concerned the CNAA's Chief Officer when he wrote his letter of 19 February 1981. There were further humiliations in October. Mr Fielden, returning from sick leave and told that his duties had been taken over, submitted a grievance; and the Chairman of Governors, announcing that the Polytechnic was now working to an establishment strictly controlled by the Authority, was at pains to assure Academic Board that its role in determining allocations of resources was inviolable. But if this was intended to isolate the Rector, he retaliated

59. Councillor C I Mernagh

spiritedly: he tabled a cutting from *The Times* to show that Huddersfield was 'in a midway position' in a table showing 'unit (per student) costs' in polytechnics.[27]

The Rector's real counter-attack came in November. He informed members at an extraordinary meeting of Academic Board that a visit had been paid to the Polytechnic, on 15 October, by a party consisting of the Under-Secretary at the DES responsible for polytechnics, Mr J Thompson; Mr E Norris, HM Chief Inspector; Mr J Nichols, of the DES; and, joining this distinguished company, 'District and General Inspector Mr A Arnison'. A minute in the Rector's own wording records that

The President of the (Students') Union reported that with the Deputy President he had had a long discussion with the Chief Inspector, Mr E Norris, who had been most complimentary about the developments of the Institution from its humble origins, and its present work. The Chief Inspector referred to the Institution being twenty paces back from being a Polytechnic when it was formed in 1970, and that to make it a Polytechnic had not been just a matter of changing the label on the door as had been the case in some institutions. The Chief Inspector had said that Huddersfield Polytechnic was a well-balanced institution doing the job which Polytechnics were intended to do, and that he had seen some good and progressive areas of work. The Rector confirmed the report given by the President of the Union.

There is no record that this oral report was discussed, or that any questions were asked about it. But the visit, and the manner of its being reported, greatly strengthened the Rector's position and marked a turning point in his relations with Councillor Mernagh.

When the Governors met, the student President 'spoke to the paper' he 'tabled', 'covering (the) meeting with Her Majesty's Chief Inspector on 15th October ...' HMI Arnison was present, and reported 'comments following the visit' which Mr Norris 'had agreed ... could be released to Governors ... which indicated that the academic standards of the institution were ... beyond reproach'.* Defensively, the Chairman remarked that there were 'doubts about relationships being as good as had been expressed to' (Mr Norris); and other Governors reported views they heard from 'national contacts' which were 'not wholly favourable'. But they could do no other than agree that any disparaging comment made about the Polytechnic 'was a misrepresentation, and failed to reflect the united effort of staff and governors towards a well ordered institution'. Mr Arnison was

---

* In January 1982 the Rector was 'authorised to release the Inspector's comments to the press'. At their February meeting the Governors asked why the statement had not yet appeared, and the Rector was required 'to give this matter urgent attention'. Despite this requirement, and the importance of this episode for the Rector's position, the 'matter' was not, apparently, raised again.[28]

asked 'to give the Chairman a written statement of his report'. The meeting was adjourned for lunch. Aptly, at the resumption, it was 'inquorate': perhaps the wind had been taken out of gubernatorial sails.

The Governors met once more in 1981, for the grievance hearing of Mr Fielden. His case was presented by one of the three solicitors who accompanied him. The Governors were 'satisfied that there was no evidence that Mr Fielden had acted incorrectly', and they 'now regard(ed) the matter as closed'. They 're-affirm(ed) the decision about the duties of the Chief Administrative Officer', and rejected 'any charge' that they had been 'intimidatory'. They requested their General Purposes Committee 'to consider further the matter, with a view to establishing a possible future role for Mr Fielden within the Polytechnic'. When Academic Board met, the Rector announced that Mr Fielden had resigned, and made no further comment.[29]

There was a less-contentious consequence of the CNAA's visit on 22 January 1981 and Dr Kerr's reporting letter of 19 February. It was to be important for the future internal organisation and academic development of the Polytechnic. As part of its response to the CNAA letter, the Academic Board had resolved that a 'working party be established to review the Board's standing committee structure, including the terms of reference of the committees and the respective roles of the Academic Board, the Standing Committees, the Rectorate, Deans and Heads of Departments'. This working party appointed as its chairman Mr N A Bastin, then head of the Division of Law. It reported to the Board in June 1981 and its recommendations ('the Bastin Report') were largely accepted, so that by the end of the year a revised committee structure was established and the roles of the senior staff and of the Board's committees and panels were defined. The Committee continued to meet, as required, and was a model of how 'roles and relationships' – at least within the Polytechnic's academic community – could be successfully defined and implemented.

60. Mr. K. J. Durrands, Rector of Huddersfield Polytechnic

Notes on Chapter 7

1. Kirklees Metropolitan Council (KMC), mins 31, 17 January 1974; 82, 25 January 1974.
2. Ac Bd 75/4, 75/21, 75/26; 75/40; 75/77; 75/86; 75/128 ('The Review of Non-Teaching Establishments - Discussion Paper', August 1975); Govs mins 75/63; 75/82; 75/59; 75/85 (January-September 1975).
3. Govs min 75/84; Ac Bd 75/139; 75/159; 75/188; 76/78; 76/114; 76/173; '7th Annual Report …', 1 April 1977, para 23. The Central Services Building was officially opened by the Duchess of Kent on 17 May 1977.
4. KMC min 172, 23 April 1976; Govs min 76/43; Ac Bd 76/90; 76/136.2.
5. Govs min 76/53; 'Relationship Between the Local Authority and the Polytechnic', 14 July 1976; Report of 'Council Visit to Huddersfield Polytechnic on 3 and 4 March 1977', CNAA, 1979, para 2.6.
6. Govs mins 76/62.2,3; Ac Bd 76/157; 76/179.4; 77/3.2.
7. Govs mins 74/122; 76/37; 77/3.2; Revised Instrument of Government, 24 January 1977; KMC min ES 135, 417, 1 February 1977; Govs mins 14 February 1977; 77/15; Ac Bd 77/46; 77/136.2; Govs min 78/72.
8. Govs min 75/82; Ac Bd 76/33; 76/116; 77/31; Govs min 77/21; KMC min 106(c)(ii), 15 December 1975; Ac Bd 77/140; 77/168; 78/37.
9. Ac Bd 76/60; 76/106; 76/140; 76/173; 77/17; 77/48.2; 77/79; 77/104; Govs min 75/05; Ac Bd 77/157; Govs min 77/30; Ac Bd 77/177, 178, 179; 78/64; Govs min 78/53.
10. Govs mins 74/83; 75/29; 75/35; 75/62. Ac Bd 75/48; 76/52; Govs min 76/16; Ac Bd 76/125; 76/131; 76/146, 160; Govs min 76/55; Ac Bd 76/168; 76/179; 77/3.1; 77/48; CNAA Report of … 3 and 4 March 1977, para. 3.5 (1979); Mins of joint meetings, 7 April 1978 - 21 April 1978.
11. Ac Bd 77/1; Govs min 77/12; Ac Bd 77/72; 77/104.5; 77/156; Govs mins 77/45; 78/3; 78/17; Ac Bd 78/77; Govs min 78/52; Ac Bd 78/154; Govs min 79/3 (b); 'Memorandum to Heads of Departments, 30 October 1979: Rector's Review of Expenditure and Policy Proposals'; Govs mins 78/74; 79/2; Ac Bd 78/158; 76/157.4; Govs mins 78/40; 78/53; Ac Bd 78/120; Govs mins 22 September 1978; Govs mins 79/16; 79/25.
12. Ac Bd 77/38, 77/45; 78/133; 79/24; HDE, 27 January 1979; CNAA Report: 'Council Visit … 3 and 4 March 1977'; Ac Bd 79/24; 79/78; 79/165; Govs min 80/27; *HDE*, 12 November 1979; 6, 7, 10, 11, 12 and 15 December 1979.
13. Govs min 78/74; 79/2; Ac Bd 79/17; 79/27; 79/72; 79/86. I am grateful to the late Mr M E Bond, Academic Registrar, for his elucidation of the Shiraz project.
14. *HDE*, Thursday, 6 December 1979; Wednesday, 11 December 1979; Govs min 79/41, 49.
15. Ac Bd 79/174; Govs min 79/56, 'Special Meeting', 20 December 1979.
16. Ac Bd 80/1; Govs mins 80/3, 4(b); 10, 11; Ac Bd 80/10; 80/28; 80/54; Govs min 80/14.
17. Ac Bd 80/61; Govs min 80/32; Govs mins 80/33; 80/36. Letter from Broomheads & Neals, signed Christopher Trippett, to Rector, 11 April 1980; Govs min 80/39.
18. AC Bd 80/60 B, C, D; Govs min 80/43 (d); Ac Bd 80/63, 80, 89. 1-4; CNAA 'Report of an Institutional Review Visit to the Polytechnic, Huddersfield on 4 and 5 March 1982, para 1.2 (21 April 1982)
19. Govs mins 80/53, 60; Ac Bd 80/91; 80/94. 1,2,3; Govs min 80/77; Ac Bd 80/114.
20. Govs mins 80/83, 84; *HDE*, 12, 18 and 19 August 1980; Govs min 80/86.
    Sir Frank Layfield had been chairman of the Enquiry into Local Government Finance, 1974-76.
21. Ac Bd 80/116-119; *HDE* 12 August 1980; Govs min 80/88(e); Ac Bd 80/121-3.
22. Govs mins 6 October 1980; Ac Bd mins 10 October 1980; Ac Bd 80/39; 80/137; 80/165, 168, 169; Govs min 80/151c; Ac Bd 80/173; Govs mins 80/149, Ac Bd 80/180, 182, 187-9, 195.
23. Govs mins 80/161, 163; Ac Bd 80/205; Govs mins 80/168, 170; KMC min C13, June-September 1980; Govs mins G/80/169.
24. Govs min 81/21; Ac Bd 81/43; Govs min 81/28; *HDE* 27 February 1981; CNAA 'Report on … visit … March 1982', para 1.5; Ac Bd 81/48, 49.
25. Govs mins 81/33; 81/35; 81/40; 81/68; 81/61; Ac Bd 81/20.
26. Govs mins 80/33; 149; Ac Bd 81/118; 122.5; 104; 119; Govs mins 81/57; 58; 67, 73; 88; 103; 111.
27. Govs mins 81/117; 81/121, KMC mins 88, 16 June 1981; Govs mins; 81/141G; 81/144; Ac Bd 81/170.
28. Govs mins 82/7; 82/24 CNAA 'Report on … visit … March 1982, para 1.9 (21.4.82).
29. Ac Bd 81/178.1; 183; Govs mins 81/164; 178; Ac Bd 81/179.4.
30. Ac Bd 81/43; 137; 149 etc. The Polytechnic, Huddersfield: 'First Report of the Working Party on Committee Structure Etc', June 1981 (Revised September 1981); 'Second Report of the Working Party on Committee Structure Etc'. (December 1981).

CHAPTER 8

VIII. Letters Patent of the Polytechnic

CHAPTER 8

ROLES, RELATIONSHIPS AND THE ROAD TO INDEPENDENCE, 1982-89

(a) Roles and Relationships, 1982-84

When they were told of Mr Fielden's resignation, the Governors decided that he should leave forthwith, without serving notice, but that he should 'be paid his full salary as Director of Academic Support Services' till 30 April 1982. Mr Durrands persuaded Academic Board, meeting on 29 January, to set up a 'Personal Representation Group', 'to listen to grievances ... of staff who ... did not feel they had fair treatment ...', and pushed it, in 'a recorded vote', to resolve 'to regret that Mr Fielden found it necessary to resign'. The Board divided: 15 were for the resolution; eight were against; seven abstained.[1] The Group reported on 'grievances and difficulties of staff' (i.e. of Mr Fielden) in March, and the Board resolved that the Rector should 'ask those concerned whether grievance and appeal procedures in the case of P Fielden have been properly and exhaustively followed'. In May the Rector paid tribute to Mr Fielden 'on his resignation', and reported on his pursuance of his case against Kirklees.[2] It was the chief of several issues on which he led the Board in a running battle, throughout 1982, with the Governors and the LEA. Others were failure to release funds and make necessary appointments, and the inefficiencies of Kirklees Technical Services. In turn, the Governors complained that the Rector did not produce 'detailed information'.[3]

These altercations exemplified the 'roles and relationships' problem, itself a facet of the marathon exercise of revising the Instrument and Articles of Government. 'Roles and relationships' figured prominently in discussions during the CNAA's 'institutional review' on 4-5 March and in the subsequent report, dated 23 April. Dr Kerr asked for a 'progress report' on them by Easter 1983 - a year ahead - and offered to mediate. The CNAA report was favourable: academic standards had not been 'harmed' by the 'relationships' difficulties; 'the overall financial problems (were) not greater than' those in 'some other institutions of higher education'; and the attitude of the Chairman of Governors had been re-assuring. When, in July, Mr Gaskell could announce that a student/staff ratio (SSR) of 10:1 would be achieved by September 1982, the ship seemed to be on an even keel. At the same meeting the Governors resolved 'that "the motion now mentioned" be withdrawn pending receipt of Sir Frank Layfield's report'. Then, in October, the words 'pending receipt of Sir Frank Layfield's report' were deleted from the minute. There ended the saga of 'the motion now mentioned'. The motion was never put to the vote, and its wording was never publicly divulged. The Layfield Report was still awaited.[4]

It had been known since August 1981 that the government intended to change the way in which polytechnics were financed. A 'National Advisory Body for Local-Authority Higher Education' (NAB) was established later that year to end the 'open-pool' system of funding. During 1982 rumours circulated about closures of courses, and in October the NAB issued a questionnaire to all public-sector institutions of higher education. Huddersfield made a return, but Governors supported Academic Board in refusing to complete a section asking for priorities to be listed in the event of reduced resources. At least they could now agree to refuse to co-operate with an external body. The Students' Union made its own, uncompromising, response, which the Governors supported, complaining that DES allocations 'effectively penalised those Polytechnics which have been prudent in their spending', a category into which Huddersfield now virtuously fell.[5] Separately from the NAB exercise, the DES made a 'provisional proposal' that the Polytechnic's courses in initial school-teacher training should end. Governors and LEA endorsed the Board's resistance, and the Kirklees Director of Educational Services visited the DES with the Rector. But this time the threat was carried out.[6]

Animosities still remained. Mr Fielden took his case for unfair dismissal to an industrial tribunal, which ruled in his favour, and then rejected a 'financial offer' by the LEA. Mr Durrands was determined to see him restored to his former position, and brought up his case at every opportunity. In January 1983 he induced the Academic Board to alter the Registrar's minuting of its November meeting to record that Governors had 'considered documents relating to Mr P H Fielden versus Kirklees MC', and to hold a special meeting to consider 'the findings of the Industrial Tribunal'. The Registrar had refused to distribute these documents, since ''the Board would be acting outside its terms of reference' in discussing 'matters ... affecting employment of a named individual'. This friction intensified in March, when the Rector over-rode the Registrar in distributing papers about the Fielden case.[7] Members agreed to consider the case at a special meeting, on 22 April, for which the Rector again distributed the papers, Mr Bond refusing to, and refusing to attend. It was resolved that 'in the best interests of the community and the

61. Polytechnic and Town Centre

62. An architect's model of the Central Services Building.

Polytechnic this Board asks that the decision of the Industrial Tribunal ... be implemented', and 'that the Governors be asked to discuss the full findings ... and decision of the Tribunal'. When the minutes of this meeting were received, it was moved that, because the matter was not the Board's business, they 'be not accepted', and then resolved that a vote on this motion be 'deferred to enable the Rector to seek the advice of the Secretary of State ...' The Rector told the next meeting that the matter 'would be discussed during the course of a visit to the DES on 11th July'. In October - five months after the vote was 'deferred' - the Board accepted an explanation by Mr Barr (in the Rector's silent presence) that, at the DES, 'officials had indicated they considered it was within the powers of the Board to discuss the matter'. With that much assurance, the Board approved the minutes of the special meeting on 22 April.[8]

Mr Fielden's position was central to relations between the Chairman and the Rector, and thus to the wider issues of 'roles and relationships' and revision of the Instrument and Articles of Government. In January 1983, Academic Board had asked Governors 'to enquire of the LEA whether the report of Sir Frank Layfield had been received, and could be made available, and, if not, when it might be expected'. Councillor Mernagh - who, after the May 1983 elections, was again Chairman of the Education Committee and the Governing Council - told Governors that the report 'was believed to be still unavailable because of Sir Frank's illness'. In July, when Pro Rector Barr was consulting the CNAA on the 'final draft of the progress report' on 'Roles and Relationships', which it had been waiting for since April 1982, the Kirklees Chief Executive sent to the Polytechnic 'amended proposals for revision of the Instrument and Articles of Government which the Local Authority had submitted to the DES'. The DES mentioned 'the Layfield enquiry' in a letter of 29 July to Kirklees about the LEA's relations with the Polytechnic, and in September the Chief Executive suggested that, while 'the Layfield Report on Huddersfield

63. View of the Polytechnic campus

Polytechnic' was 'still awaited', 'a joint committee' from Governors and the Education Committee should 'be established to prepare a statement on the ... relationships' between Polytechnic and Education Authority. That was the last recorded mention of the 'Layfield Report', three years after the enquiry began. A report was produced, but it was never published.*[9]

In December 1983 the NAB announced allocations to polytechnics and colleges of numbers of students they would be allowed to recruit, in designated 'programme areas', in 1984-5. The NAB had by now become a common enemy helping to bind together Rectorate, Board, Governors and Authority, though, ironically, it was to be one agent making for the ending of Local Authority oversight of higher education.[10] Annual battles over financial allocations between the Polytechnic and Kirklees were things of the past, though the Polytechnic still complained about late release of funds and the Authority's retention of 'contingency' money. In March 1983 the Governors supported the Academic Board's pressing request to Kirklees for 'release of a further £363,000 from contingency and to authorise necessary virement' to ensure its optimum use. Despite the frictions - and the Fielden case apart - working relations were approaching normality. The Governors supported the Polytechnic's purposes: promoting new courses in technology; providing better staffing of computer services; creating a Law department; establishing a professoriat. The Rector told the last Governors' meeting of 1983 that, 'according to (NAB) statistics, the Polytechnic was an economical institution'. Another measure of the

---

* The fate of the 'Layfield Report on Huddersfield Polytechnic' is concealed from the records. A draft was produced, and submitted to the Kirklees Chief Executive and Mr Durrands for comment. It is clear that neither the Rector nor Councillor Mernagh was displeased that it was not published. 'Sir Frank's illness' - given to the Governors by their Chairman, on 4 February 1983, as a reason for the delay in the report's appearance - must have been a short one, and is not a credible explanation of why there is no 'Layfield Report'. From 1983 to 1985 Sir Frank presided over the 'Enquiry into Sizewell B Nuclear Power Station', and a report on that was published.

64. Sir Harold Wilson, Rector Kenneth J Durrands and Councillor John Mernagh at the opening of the 'Firth Street Building', May 1983

transformation was that since 1981 the FTE number of academic staff had fallen by 100 and the FTE numbers of students had risen by 470, so that the student/staff ratio had risen from 8.1:1 in 1980-81 to 10.8:1 in 1983-84.[11]

From October 1983 a 'Joint Committee' (of Governors, Academic Board and LEA) on 'Roles and Relationships' met. Mr Barr, who represented the Board, kept it informed of the Committee's progress. He reported improving working relationships: 'it was particularly pleasing that the (Kirklees) Director of Finance and the Rector were making joint reports to Governors'. Nationally, there were changes during 1984 in polytechnics' relationships to their academic regulators, the NAB and the CNAA. The NAB was made permanent in May, and the CNAA's role was under scrutiny. Polytechnic Directors, anxious to raise their institutions' status, saw self-validation of courses as one main means, and greater financial independence as the other. Kirklees supported the Association of Metropolitan Authorities when it made representations to the government for 'more equitable funding' (in comparison with universities) for the polytechnics. Yet, again, the consequence of such a trend would be independence of polytechnics from their LEAs.[12]

The most important academic initiative of 1984 was the appointment of the Polytechnic's first professors. Six senior academics were internally appointed to this non-salaried status in May, and a further four in September. In October 'the Chairman and Secretary of the Committee of External Members of the Professorial Conferment Board', Professor C Adamson and HMI Arnison, informed the Registrar 'that their Committee had strongly recommended that the Rector and Pro Rector Barr should have the title Professor

65. Ramsden Building interior

conferred on them', and the Conferment Board had 'unanimously adopted' the recommendation. Academic Board congratulated the teams that gained approval for the Polytechnic's first MBA course. This was its second taught Master's course, the first having been an MA in History, approved in 1976 and successfully taught since then. Two other initiatives of 1984 had lasting effects. A group of HMI had visited polytechnics to investigate the perennial problem of recruitment to engineering courses. Huddersfield's governors discussed their report on three occasions, and the Engineering Faculty promoted a 'Technology Foundation Course for Women', for which, it was hoped, there would be funding from the European Social Fund.[13] The other venture was the launching of the Huddersfield Contemporary Music Festival. For this, the Governors were asked to allow use of 'certain Polytechnic facilities (principally St Paul's Hall, as it had been named since 1981) to be used free of charge'. Assured that Academic Board 'could see no objection to these requests', Governors agreed. No one involved in this seemingly back-handed endorsement can have imagined what this initiative would become. Only two years later, the Registrar was asked to convey to Richard Steinitz, the festival's organiser, 'the Board's appreciation of the great benefits (brought) to the Polytechnic and locality by the Contemporary Music Festival'.[14]

(b) Evolution to Independence, 1985-89

The Polytechnic had two important visitors in March 1985: Sir Norman Lindop and Mr Christopher Ball. Sir Norman was much the more welcome. His report, 'Academic Validation of Degree Courses in Public-Sector Higher Education', recommending self-validation as and when polytechnics proved themselves ready for it, had just been published. At the time, Huddersfield was corresponding with the CNAA on how the Council's new 'Partnership in Validation' policy should be applied, and suggesting self-validation for itself by September 1986. In contrast, relations with the National Advisory Body (NAB), the funding body, of whose Board Mr Ball was Chairman, were contested at every stage: about its allocations of numbers and funds for 1986-7; and its 'restrictive' proposals for 1987-8. As Professor Barr explained to Governors in July, 1985 was proving to be a year of 'major planning initiatives'. As well as the Lindop Report, there had been published the government's Green Paper on higher education into the next decade, and there was to be a NAB report on management of the polytechnics, which were now expected to have plans for 'commercial enterprise and entrepreneurial activities'.[15] Challenged by these national pressures, Professor Durrands produced in October a 'Review of the Development ... and Consideration of Future Policy and Organisation of the Polytechnic'. It set as targets greater autonomy from the LEA; from the NAB, an increase in student numbers, 'to raise the student/staff ratio to NAB norms';

66. St. Paul's interior view

and from the CNAA agreement to 'the highest level of self-validation'. Longer-term aims were to set up 'an enterprise agency with limited liability', expansion of 'continuing' and 'in-service education and training' and improvement of 'overseas student recruitment'. Finally, 'the Institution should consider ... whether it should apply to change its name to either "University" or "University-Polytechnic" '.[16]

The document showed that relations with Kirklees had much improved. This improvement was marked by a change in Councillor Mernagh's position. It resulted partly from his own mis-judgement. There had been a student demonstration during a ministerial visit to the Polytechnic in March. Councillor Mernagh put a motion to Governors that, 'arising from the Home Secretary's visit ...', there should be 'no further visits without the consent of the Governing Body'. He lost face by having to withdraw his motion 'in the light of the Academic Board minute' that such visits should take place, even though there might be 'dislocation of the teaching programme'. In July, in a secret ballot, he was defeated in the annual election for Chairman by Mr R C Cross, the trade unionist. Councillor Mrs Carter was elected Vice-Chairman, but, at the next meeting, after 'a short adjournment', 'the Clerk announced her decision to resign' and Councillor Mernagh became Vice-Chairman.[17] By the end of 1985 co-operation between the Polytechnic and Kirklees was the norm. The Governors noted with pleasure a resolution of Kirklees MC 'that this Council, recognising the value of higher education in the economy of Britain, deplores the closure of the School of Architecture at Huddersfield Polytechnic; and, acknowledging the contribution of the Polytechnic to the cultural, educational and economic life of Kirklees, pledges to oppose any further threat to its size or functions'. Correcting the Council's factual error, the Governors thanked it for its support against the 'proposed closure' of Architecture.[18]

Initiatives to expand student recruitment were all the more needed in the new entrepreneurial culture. The 'Technology Foundation Course for Women' was launched, with EU funding, and re-training courses in industry and commerce under the 'PICKUP' scheme received DES grants. The Polytechnic was a beneficiary of an 'Engineering and Technology Programme' financed by the NAB, which was some compensation for its alleged 'inequitable' research funding.[19] Overseas connections were fostered. The Academic Board welcomed Professor J-F Robert, President of the Université de Franche Comté at Besançon, in March 1985, and from his visit developed student exchanges and

67. Harold Wilson on a visit to the Polytechnic

research seminars in Chemistry, as they also did with the polytechnic-university at Lannion, Brittany. Professor Robert was to be made a Fellow of the Polytechnic in 1988. Important for the future, too, was an invitation from the British Council to bid for a contract to train Indonesian students.[20]

On the campus, the students began a campaign for the re-housing of their Union, from the former St Joseph's school, which they had occupied since 1968. When a proposal was made, in May, for a move to 'the old Administration Block', otherwise the 'Great Hall' building, and the Union applied to Kirklees for a loan, the Governors approved the move 'in principle', provided the costs were borne by the Union. But the proposal had serious accommodation implications for the Polytechnic, and the Rector had Academic Board's support in wanting 'flexibility' about the agreement.[21]

Of the 'major planning initiatives', those which had immediate effects were the Lindop Report, affecting relations with the CNAA, and the NAB's planning project for 1987-8. The outcome of a visit by a NAB officer, in February 1986, was pleasantly surprising: reductions in student-number allocations from what the Polytechnic had optimistically proposed were less than expected, and did not threaten the continuance of any course except Architecture. The Polytechnic's main business with the CNAA was to reach an agreement on 'partnership in validation'. Proposals had to be submitted by Easter 1986, and a draft was prepared with help from CNAA officers. The results of an enquiry which the Association of Metropolitan Authorities (AMA) had sponsored into the costs of CNAA validation of polytechnic courses strengthened the case for self-validation.[22] With Kirklees, negotiations on 'roles and relationships' still limped on in 1986, but working relations were progressively easier. The Authority's capital allocation to the Polytechnic for 1986-7 was more than the DES had recommended, and it was thanked for its financial support. Monitoring of revenue expenditure still went on, but rather as a formality, and with mutual trust. So, too, did the joint reporting by the Rector and the Kirklees Finance Director on current expenditure and capital planning.[23]

A threat of closure had hung over the School of Architecture since September 1985, when HM Inspectors proposed it, following a national survey of student places. Governors and LEA supported the Polytechnic's case for retaining its teaching; there were student demonstrations; the Regional Advisory Council and the Yorkshire branch of the RIBA gave support. Amid rejoicing, the Rector announced in December that the NAB's

Committee had rejected the closure proposal. But the DES, advising the Secretary of State, had to be persuaded. Letters were sent to Sir Keith Joseph from Governors, LEA, AMA and RIBA, and visits made to his Department. In March 1986 the LEA was notified that the DES proposed that there be no new intake to Architecture at Huddersfield in September. As well as a further LEA/Polytechnic delegation, there was lobbying of the Secretary of State by local MPs; and Wakefield Council and the lecturers' union, NATFHE, protested. But on 16 June the DES confirmed to Kirklees and some other 'maintaining Authorities' that their Architecture departments could not recruit in September.[24] At this point, Professor Barr informed Governors how, as a member of a joint-LEA delegation, he had received advice from a QC that the Polytechnic should seek a legal review and that an affidavit was being prepared, seeking 'an investigation into the way in which the NAB arrived at its decision to recommend closure of the Part I' RIBA course. Kirklees was joined by the London Borough of Newham (the LEA of North-East London Polytechnic).[*] The application for judicial review failed, and the appellants were ordered to pay costs. The DES then informed the Polytechnic that 'the Minister' would give approval for a Part I course to be taught to overseas students only. An attempt was made to raise an entry, but 'an intake of sufficient size and quality' could not be recruited, and the Board supported a proposal that approval should be sought to develop courses in 'building and construction studies'.[25]

68. Harold Wilson at the Polytechnic – a study in musical appreciation. The author is second from the left

The NAB system was an exercise in planning: to control the numbers of students entering subject ('programme') areas in public-sector higher education. Outside the system were overseas students, on whose behalf full-cost fees were paid, and who were additional to allocations. The Polytechnic continued to recruit them successfully. In January 1986 Professor Barr told Governors that the Indonesian project had succeeded: students would start their engineering course in September. There were many alarms and delays before, on 31 October - six weeks into term - Academic Board approved a re-structured course to meet their needs. By Christmas a second Indonesian contract was announced, for a three-year course, to be taught at Holly Bank, to train teachers in secondary-technical schools.[26]

---

[*] Whose course was also to be closed, and whose Director was Mr G T Fowler, Assistant Director at Huddersfield, 1970-72.

69. St Paul's Hall

Where they could be, academic initiatives at home were taken. The Polytechnic applied to become an 'accredited centre' for the training of instructors on the government's Youth Training Scheme, and Governors were alerted to the possible effect on the Polytechnic's in-service training of teachers ('INSET') of a new funding system which the DES intended to introduce from April 1987. The Kirklees LEA was urged to recognise the Polytechnic's claim to bid for whatever INSET work the Authority decided to commission, and the Polytechnic aimed to extend its in-service work to embrace as wide a range of teachers as possible. Its ambition to secure the training of Kirklees school teachers had been made possible by the restoration to it of 'initial' training of school teachers in specified 'shortage subjects' during the year.[27] Other initiatives related to the government's training agency, the Manpower Services Commission (MSC). In April Pro Rector Gaskell proposed to Governors an arrangement, initially for one year, for the Polytechnic to become an accredited centre for the MSC.[28]

The Polytechnic was intent on increasing the effectiveness of staff as teachers, and encouraging their research activities. A new system of staff-development appraisal, which Heads of Departments were to implement, was introduced. In February 1986, a survey of teaching methods was conducted, and a report presented to Academic Board which members described as 'excellent', and which was distributed to all staff. Professor M S Burnip, Dean of Research, dispensed a fund to support individuals' research or study for further qualifications, and, unwittingly reviving an old tradition, he issued a record of 'Research in Progress and Staff Publications' for the year 1984-5, intending it to be an annual publication.[29] Such measures were seen as part of the 'enterprise culture' which the Rector had promoted in his 'Review'. A proposal to establish a 'Polytechnic Enterprise Agency' was accepted 'in principle' in January 1986, to be headed by an Assistant Rector. The appointment of Dr P F Arthur, from April 1987, was to add a

70. Queensgate Campus temporary building

fourth member to the Rectorate, and from the start of the new academic year in September 1986 there were changes at Dean of Faculty level. Three of the five Deans were replaced.[30]

For officers of the Students' Union, 1986 was a frustrating year in their efforts to find a new home. Under pressure from the student President, the Governors set a date - September 1987 - for the Union's occupation of the Great Hall building. But Academic Board was alarmed at the consequent loss of the Polytechnic's main examinations hall, and there was no funding to re-house the administrative staff who would be ejected from their building for the Union to occupy it. The Rector was asked to prepare a 'corporate' capital plan by the end of the year,[31] but to the students this was a dragging-out of the process.

The tormented Sir Keith Joseph was succeeded as Secretary of State for Education and Science, in May 1986, by Kenneth Baker. He planned to visit Huddersfield Polytechnic in January 1987, but bad weather intervened and the visit was never made. Perhaps Mr Baker was too busy planning his April White Paper and the 'Great Education Reform Bill' ('GERBIL'), to be published in November. More-immediate national developments affecting the Polytechnic were summarised by the Rector for Academic Board in March: initiatives coming from the Manpower Services Commission (MSC); the 'Open College' idea; new vocational qualifications (NCVQ) and 'INSET' arrangements; moves towards 'modularisation' of courses; 'private-sector' involvement in higher education and the willingness of the Business and Technical Education Council (BTEC) to accredit 'modules' taken in industry.[32] The White Paper, *Higher Education: Meeting the Challenge*, and a DES document on changes in the structure and national planning of public-sector higher education - to which the LEA and Polytechnic were to reply jointly - were discussed by Governors and Academic Board from May onwards. Their implications were profound: 'corporate status' for the polytechnics; and the extension of access to higher education and hence a steep increase in student numbers. But the independence from the LEA of 'corporate status' would mean that the Polytechnic could no longer rely on the Authority's 'topping up' of income from its non-advanced work; and if the Polytechnic was to live within its means another large-scale premature-retirement scheme would be necessary, the implementation of which would depend on the goodwill of the Authority.[33]

Besides financial implications - involving relations with the NAB, as well as Kirklees - there were academic consequences of corporate status, which affected the CNAA/Polytechnic relationship. In March 1987 the Polytechnic applied to the CNAA for 'institutional accreditation'. This was a step towards complete self-validation, beyond the course-by-course accreditation given by the 'partnership in validation' that the Council had approved for Huddersfield only in February. A fourth quinquennial 'institutional review', postponed in 1986, was now arranged for February 1988, and was to be combined with an 'accreditation' visit.[34]

The most immediate impact of the White Paper and the publication of the Education Bill was on the Polytechnic's relations with Kirklees. The amicably-agreed revenue budget for 1987-8 - the penultimate year of financing under LEA regulation - amounted to £24,260,000, which included a rate-fund contribution of £2,190,000. The Governors urged the Authority to ensure that the Polytechnic 'derived maximum benefit from ... further allocations' by the Department of Trade and Industry (DTI) and the DES to purchase textile machinery valued at over £200,000. They did this because such

71. Engineering Tower and Z Block. Z Block is so named because it is one arm of a covered walkway linking the Chemistry building with the Central Services Building

72. Catering Building

allocations were conditional on the LEA's matching the ministries' grants. The DTI had also included Huddersfield among 'a number of selective Universities' (*sic*) in a 'collaborative project' being discussed, under which the Department would provide capital funding of £250,000 which 'would enable the Polytechnic to upgrade its mainframe (computer) facilities'. Definitions of roles and relationships were now irrelevant: future relations with Kirklees would be about the Polytechnic's co-operation in schemes like 'Kirklees as an Engine of Growth' and 'Tourism Strategy'.[35]

On the internal academic front, the state of the School of Architecture became perilous. In the immediate future, the School would have to depend on its HND-level work, and on 'consolidating the Graduate Diploma course', which was a self-validated Polytechnic award. 1987 ended with the dismal news that the NAB was pressing for a response to a new DES proposal that the School's remaining work for the RIBA qualification should cease. The only glimmer of hope was that the Royal Institute supported the Polytechnic's case for its retention.[36]

The failure to recruit Architecture students from overseas was consistent with a quiet year in other areas of attempted recruitment from abroad. A staff visit to Hong Kong did not produce students. Nor did the British Council's bid for a second contract with Indonesia, for 'the upgrading of secondary-technical teachers', or its project 'to upgrade four Nigerian Polytechnics'. In December Professor Barr announced the establishment of 'formal links in the field of electrical engineering with Charles University, Prague, a leading university in Europe'. Indeed it was, but the links proved to be tenuous. Those with Malawi Polytechnic were stronger, and Professor Barr suggested that the recent death of its principal 'should be marked in some way' at Huddersfield.[37]

Nearer home, various forms of industrial liaison were fostered. An MSC Accredited Centre was set up, to be operated and monitored for a year from April 1987, and a teaching-company partnership received a grant of £130,425 from the Science and

73. Catering Building

Engineering Research Council (SERC). But the established Centre for Industrial and Educational Liaison (CIEL) was a continuing drain, and had to be wound up in May 1989, leaving the new Higher Education Corporation to settle its outstanding debts and absorb its redundant staff.[38] External funding for the PICKUP project was ended at Easter 1987, and it was financed thereafter from Polytechnic funds. Two other engineering teaching programmes promised to be more lucrative. The MSC located a 'Graduate Enterprise Programme' for the Yorkshire and Humberside region at Huddersfield, and the DTI made it a training centre for its 'AMIE' (Advanced Manufacturer in Electronics) qualification. Dr Arthur became a secretary to the local enterprise initiative, 'Huddersfield 2000', and the Rector joined its Board. Engineering education was again the subject of a national initiative in 1987, when the Engineering Council began a two-year investigation, using Huddersfield as one of its nine higher-education institutions.[39]

The raising of target student numbers intensified accommodation problems. It was confirmed that the Students' Union would move into the Great Hall building on 4 April 1987. That date was passed before the President of the Union could present to Governors a request that they make a loan to finance the re-furbishment needed, 'if the Polytechnic became an independent corporate body, and assuming the Local Authority could not continue to act as guarantor'. The Governors supported the proposal 'in principle', and subject to their receiving favourable legal advice. There the matter remained when the Education Bill was published in November. By then, the Union was campaigning on a new issue. In May, the Polytechnic began a drive to extend 'access' to its courses to 'non-standard entrants', mainly mature students. Academic Board supported the Union's campaign for 'subsidised nursery provision', accepting it as an 'essential aid to recruitment'. Governors were more cautious: they asked for information about costing. Surprisingly, the students did not complain about their poor sports facilities: it was left to

74. Workshop Block

the Board's Welfare Committee to draw unfavourable comparisons with 'recreational facilities' at other Yorkshire polytechnics.[40]

Union problems apart, a 'crisis in Polytechnic accommodation' was declared. In a meeting with Kirklees, in May 1987, Mr Gaskell outlined proposals for financing the 'second phase' of adaptations to Albany Mills for Polytechnic use, and possibly acquiring other properties in Firth Street. There was also costly repair work to the Chemistry building and Textiles workshops, and at Holly Bank. 'In view of the anticipated increase in student numbers', there was a shortage of 'hall accommodation'. But there was a 'national moratorium on capital funds for student residences for a number of years' ahead, and the only means of bringing immediate relief was by buying more houses.[41]

As soon as the Education Reform Bill was published, in November 1987, preparations began for the 'vesting day' of 'The Polytechnic of Huddersfield Higher Education Corporation' (HEC), 1 April 1989. Kirklees Councillors could only accept their loss of power, and offer the advice they thought necessary. The Education Committee warned that there was 'no basis for paying any expenses to (Governors) in connection with their attendance at meetings of the Governing Body or its sub-committees'. In June 1988 a 'Formation Committee', an embryonic Governing Body, was formed, with seven members: Councillor Jane Carter; Messrs R C Cross and N Haigh, respectively Chairman and Vice-Chairman of the existing Governing Body; Dr J S Hughes, a consultant psychiatrist, who had been consultant to students; one staff member, Mr R van Kemenade; Mr B Ward, a chartered accountant; and the Rector. The Academic Board unsuccessfully urged that 'the Governors ... include one person appointed by the Academic Board in their full membership'. When the Board received proposed Articles of Government for the Corporation, members 'reiterated' their concern about an article

75. Workshop Block

that required the Board to seek the permission of 'the Governors and the Principal' before it set up its own committees. In response, the Rector 'invited members to make written depositions to him on any points that caused them concern', but warned that they had less than a week in which to do this.[42]

For its first meeting, in December, the Formation Committee had been expanded to include five more members: Mr N A Bastin and Mr H Driver, elected to represent teaching and non-teaching staff, respectively; Councillor J A Harman, who represented Kirklees Council, of which he was newly-elected Labour Leader; and two additional members appointed by 'the Corporation', Mrs K Hill and Mr P H Fielden, the former Director of Academic Support Services ('DASS'). The first items of business were to elect to the newly-designated offices of 'President' and 'Vice-President'. Mr Cross - while remaining Chairman of the existing body - and Mrs Carter, who resigned her position on Kirklees Council to become eligible, were elected. The office of 'President' was a recommendation of the Academic Board, accepting the Rector's suggestion that 'a post akin to a University Chancellorship' should be created. It also revived the original title of the Institution's Chairman, and had had a previous resurrection between 1972 and 1974. This meeting accepted a proposal that Professor Colin Adamson, former Director of the Polytechnic of Central London and in 1976-7 adviser to Mr Durrands on possible limited-company status for Huddersfield Polytechnic, be submitted to the DES for nomination as 'the Governor with experience of Higher Education'. Joining Professor Barr 'in attendance' at this meeting was Mr C D Trippett, the solicitor who had advised the Rector in the crisis of 1980-81. He modestly withdrew when the appointment of legal advisers to the new Corporation was discussed. It was explained that the Governors needed legal advice on drafting Articles of Government which had to be submitted to the DES, and on the transfer of assets from the Local Authority. Not surprisingly, at a

76. Warrenfield – student accommodation

meeting in March, Mr Trippett's firm was 'confirmed' in its appointment as the Corporation's solicitors.[43] Provisional appointments were also made of bankers, auditors and insurance brokers, and it was resolved to establish a 'Secretariat to serve the new Corporation and the Rectorate'. Approval was given to appoint a Head of Secretariat, who 'would be Secretary of the Council'.

Academic Board had been told that 'the Secretary of State had issued a severe prescription for the content of Articles' of Government, but members complained that a section of the model articles, on academic freedom, had been excluded from the version presented to Governors; and they repeated their earlier complaint about the omission of Board representation on the Governing Council.[44] The Council appointed two committees: an Audit Committee, of which Mr Ward became Chairman; and a Management Committee - later, General Purposes Committee - of which the President was a member, but, crucially, Mr Fielden was Chairman. Two items at this first meeting defied the unequivocal advice given by Kirklees. The first, consideration of the payment of travelling and subsistence allowances to Council members, was 'deferred'. When the second, payment of honoraria, was raised, the Rector was asked to seek legal advice.[45] This subject was not raised again, but 'travelling and subsistence allowances' was to be a persistent item of Council agenda until March 1991, when the two staff members moved that 'expenditure figures arising from members' travelling and subsistence claims' be published. Their motion was defeated and the matter seemingly then closed.[46]

Three other meetings of the Corporation's Governing Council were held, in 1989, before it replaced the retiring Governing Body on 1 April. Membership was extended for the second meeting, in January, to include Lord Gregson, an industrialist, and the President of the Students' Union; and for the third, in February, to include Professor C Adamson-

77. Z Block

Macedo, as he was now named. There were then 15 members, and consideration of increased Local Authority and Academic Board representation was indefinitely 'deferred'. These early-1989 meetings dealt mainly with transfer of assets and of responsibilities from Kirklees MC to the new Corporation. The value of the Polytechnic's buildings was estimated to be £70m, and that of equipment £20m. The new Management Committee was 'anxious' that the Rector should be authorised to 'call on the services of management consultants, should he need to', and the Governing Council resolved that 'professional help and advice be obtained to prepare the Corporate Plan' required by the new funding authority which was to replace the NAB: the Polytechnics and Colleges Funding Council (PCFC). The Rector told the Governing Council that the NAB's system of allocation had restricted student numbers, and that that was why student/staff ratios in the Polytechnic were low. He hoped the new system would allow it 'to grow out of these difficulties and ... maintain its wide spectrum of courses'.[47]

The new Council took over items from the retiring Governing Body's agenda, like re-location of the Students' Union and provision of subsidised nursery education for students' children. It approved the revenue and capital budgets for 1989-90, drawn up by Polytechnic officers, but accompanied by a 'budget review' by accountants Deloitte, Haskins and Sells. It approved a contract for the conversion of Larchfield Mill; approved the setting-up of an 'operating company' as a separate subsidiary of the Polytechnic, to save tax while preserving the charitable status of the Corporation; and transferred the Polytechnic's business projects to the new ownership. The Council had also, in recognition of their greater responsibilities, agreed to salary rises for 'the Rectorate'.[48]

The Polytechnic's last financial year under the NAB/Local Authority dispensation was a

78. Longley Park Student Residence site

particularly difficult one. Serious cuts in the 'staffing lines' of the budget for 1988-9 had to be made, and Mr Gaskell anticipated further cuts of £1.5m for 1989-90. Drastic measures were needed. The possibility of raising fee levels for part-time and for 'full-cost' students was to be investigated. But there was a great 'spending excess' on staffing, and mostly academic staffing. £1.5m represented 75 academic staff at average salary. Huddersfield was operating at a lower student/staff ratio (SSR) than the other polytechnics, and staff reductions had to be made immediately, because the new régime would also mean that the Authority's customary 'topping-up' exercises would be 'phased out over the next two years'. The only way to bring about the needed reduction in expenditure and still fulfil the teaching programme was through a scheme which would 'enable (early-) retired staff to be re-appointed on a part-time basis'. That would contradict the avowed purpose and undermine the justification of early retirement/ redundancy with enhanced pension, and Kirklees was careful to lay down conditions when it agreed to the Governors' request. They amounted to saying it must be the only means 'to prevent students being disadvantaged'. On that basis, Mr Gaskell could present proposals for achieving the necessary reduction in staffing costs in the 1988-9 and 1989-90 financial years. Even so, Huddersfield's allocation to Library expenditure in 1988-9, for instance, was the lowest among the polytechnics. At a time when some courses were moving towards 'open learning', it was forecast that the Library Services - though as well as the book collection, now grown to 300,000, it included a range of information systems unimaginable 20 years before - would not be adequate to sustain such methods.[49]

Ways to 'maximise student numbers' had to be found. The Rector told Academic Board in February 1989 that a case must be made to the PCFC for the Polytechnic to be allowed to grow immediately by at least 1,000 students if it was to sustain its current 'spectrum of courses' at viable levels. The 'spectrum' included 'lower-level' work, 'FE' courses, as

79. Milton Building entrance

well as 'HE' courses. Kirklees confirmed that it would continue to pay the fees of its students on the traditional lower-level courses, in Art and Textiles, and now students on the 'Women into Technology' course. To the final meeting of the Board under the old régime, on 23 March 1989, it was reported that notices had been received from the PCFC about its subject 'programmes', about the quality of teaching and about 'funding choices'. It was the final meeting, too, for a number of senior staff whose retirement marked an exodus even more drastic than that of 1981. Their leaving was part of a movement that brought about a reduction in the full-time-equivalent (FTE) number of academic staff from 522 to 439 over two years.[50]

The visit of the CNAA party for the fourth 'Institutional Review', and to consider the Polytechnic's application for 'institutional accreditation' had been arranged for 17-18 February 1988. Pre-visit confidence had been justified. The Council's representatives 'were very impressed with the changes made since the last Review and ... felt' that the Polytechnic was 'an academic community working well together'. Dr Kerr, the Chief Officer, hoped that 'the spirit of community' would help the Polytechnic to face the difficulties of its financial position 'arising from loss of topping up'. He was confident that there would be 'an Institutional drive' behind the changes that were now needed in the Polytechnic's academic structure and its 'teaching and learning strategies'. There would, too, have to be more systematic training and development of staff, both academic and non-teaching. 'Institutional approval' - to continue teaching for CNAA awards - was instantaneous, and 'accreditation' was announced on 24 March. The formal 'Instrument of Accreditation', making the Polytechnic responsible for its own standards in awarding CNAA Bachelors' degrees - but not yet research degrees - was announced by the CNAA in a national press release. There were thanks for the business and industrial support received, and congratulations on 'this significant achievement'.[51]

The Rector had first spoken of 'moves towards modularisation of courses' in early 1987, as one of the 'current developments nationally' that would affect the Polytechnic. In October, Academic Board accepted a proposal of the Yorkshire and Humberside Credit Accumulation and Transfer ('CAT') consortium, of which the Polytechnic was a member, for member institutions to recognise, 'subject to safeguards', success on all others' 'access' courses as entry qualifications to their own courses. A group had been set up in the Polytechnic to examine the feasibility and desirability of 'CAT'. It was being forecast that this would become universal practice, and asserted that enterprising institutions should be in a position to meet the demand. In July 1988 the group's proposal that credit accumulation and transfer should operate within the Polytechnic was agreed by the Board, to be implemented forthwith. Then, in December, the Board accepted a recommendation of the regional group that the possibility of establishing awards in 'combined studies', to be gained by CAT across institutions, should be considered. The other would-be trail-blazing idea of 1987 - the 'Open College', later named 'Open Polytechnic' - proved abortive.[52]

80. Library Information Desk

As the Rector repeated, the Polytechnic would struggle 'to sustain its current spectrum of courses at viable levels'. Architecture, of course, needed special support. But its fortunes improved decisively in 1988. The Polytechnic's response to the NAB's invitation to state its case against the recommendation that all of its Architecture teaching should cease was submitted at the end of January. There was then a *volte-face* on the part of the NAB: it decided to 'advise the Secretary of State' that the RIBA course should not be withdrawn. The supportive outside bodies - Kirklees, Calderdale and Wakefield Councils; the Royal Institute, and especially its Yorkshire branch - were thanked. The Secretary of State acted on the new advice, and the Governors congratulated the Rector and the staff concerned on 'achieving maintenance of the present position ...', and thereby, as it turned out, of the teaching of Architecture in the institution.[53]

'Enterprise' in the narrower sense, of 'business projects', met with some success, if hard-won. In January 1988, with a grant from the SERC, the Polytechnic set up its third 'Teaching Company', and in June it bid successfully to become a Training Agency. This added to the range of 'business projects' that Dr Arthur listed for the new Governing Council at its meeting in January 1989: consultancies, short courses, 'market-orientated centres' and 'special initiatives in education and training', all of them, it was hoped, income-generating activities, though often complex and expensive in the ways they did their generating. It was then time to make submissions for funding under a second round of the Training Agency's 'Enterprise in Higher Education' programme. This was the state of involvement in 'enterprises' when the Higher Education Corporation was instituted.[54]

Prominent among the problems inherited by the Corporation were the acquisition and conversion of accommodation. Mr Gaskell gave the old Governing Body a progress report in January 1988. He was then involved in negotiating the contract for the third stage of conversion of the Larchfield mill, across Firth Street from the campus, and was congratulated by the Governors for successfully completing involved negotiations so that conversion could begin in June.⁵⁵ The Students' Union had promoted its case for subsidised nursery provision since mid-1987. In March 1988 the Governors were presented with a proposal that they should pay an annual subsidy of £35,000 to provide 20 child-care places at a privately-run nursery. They contrived to draw out negotiations until they could pass on the problem to the new Governing Council. Only in February 1989 did the new Governors receive papers explaining how 'the present Governors' had handled this student request. They declared themselves 'wary' about 'the use of PCFC funding monies' for such a purpose. They approved the private-nursery proposal 'in principle', but asked for a detailed estimate of costs, 'validated by the Head of Financial Services'. The primary business for the Union was housing itself: it still had to find a way of raising the money to refurbish the Great Hall building. In April 1988 the Governors had accepted the principles set out in a letter from Kirklees officers, that the Union should become a limited company and 'enter into a licence' with the Authority. After reflection, it was realised that '… further legal advice' was needed. By February 1989, this matter, too, was in the lap of the new Governing Council. The Rector presented to it an *aide-mémoire* on 'the re-location of the Students' Union', and asked for 'urgent action'. The Council resolved that 'the possibility of identifying the capital and subsequent funding available … be explored with the PCFC in the first instance'.⁵⁶

In the quinquennium 1984-5 to 1989-90 the number of students in all categories on higher-education courses at the Polytechnic rose from 6,500 to almost 7,800; the full-time-equivalent (FTE) number rose by 1,000 to 6,250. The FTE number of academic staff fell by 40, to 439, so that the student/staff ratio (SSR) rose from 10.8:1 to 13.2:1. A calculation of the total annual running costs of the higher-education courses shows a rise over these years from £17.595m to £28.283m.⁵⁷ This expansion, at a rate averaging about 3 per cent per annum, was maintained over 'the good spectrum of courses' - across advanced ('AFE') and non-advanced ('NAFE') further education - that the Rector again told the Governing Council in March 1989 he 'wished to maintain'.

81. Moving the Library

Notes on Chapter 8

1. Govs min 82/8; Ac Bd 82/8.
2. Ac Bd 82/28; 82/36.
3. Ac Bd 82/112; Govs mins 82/130; 82/146; 82/149-169, 171; Ac Bd 82/54, 56, 67; 82/71; Govs min 82/146; Ac Bd 82/101.
4. Govs min 82/20; Ac Bd 82/9; 82/27; 82/43; 82/52; CNAA: 'Report ... 4 and 5 March 1982: Summary, paras 1.5, 2.3, 3.4; Govs mins 82/87; 82/109; Ac Bd 82/27; 82/62; 82/82; 82/79; 94.2; Govs mins 82/121; 82/124.
5. Ac Bd 82/47; Govs min 82/118; Ac Bd 82/81, 94.3; 92/99; Govs min 82/163; Ac Bd 82/111; Govs min 82/180; Ac Bd 83/5; Govs min 83/10.
6. Ac Bd 82/68; Govs mins 82/122; 82/126; KMC min 202, 31 August 1982; 254, 13 November 1982; 396, 7 December 1982; 449, 11 January 1983; Ac Bd 82/30; 92/109; Govs min 82/172.
7. Ac Bd 83/37.3; Govs min 82/181; Ac Bd 82/110; 83/1; 83/11.2. (There were three drafts of the minutes of this meeting, on 28 January 1983). Ac Bd 83/20.2. (There were four drafts of the minutes of this meeting, on 18 March 1983).
8. Ac Bd 83/37; 83/44; 83/61.2; 83/79.2.
9. KMC min E4, July-November 1983; Ac Bd 83/11; 83/17.4; Govs min 83/13; Ac Bd 82/43, 53; 83/20, 36; Govs min 93/32; Ac Bd 893/43/4, 49; 83/61.1, 5; 83/69; KMC min E81, 6 September 1983; Govs min 83/108.
10. Ac Bd 83/79.3; 83/92.1; Govs mins 83/109; 83/121; 83/107; Ac Bd 83/85; KMC min E92, 311, 11 October 1983; Ac Bd 83/92.4; 83/109; Govs min 83/120; Ac Bd 83/94.
11. Ac Bd 83/10; 83/26, 24; 83/40(a); Govs min 83/105; Ac Bd 83/62; Govs min 83/87; 83/110; KMC min E157, 541, 14 February 1984; Ac Bd 83/92.2; 83/128; Govs min 83/123.
12. Ac Bd 84/2.1; Govs min 84/9; Ac Bd 84/25; Govs mins 84/38; 84/44; 84/58; Govs min 84/89(ii); Ac Bd 84/77; 84/93; 84/25; 84/1; 84/21; 84/106; 84/5; Govs mins 84/38; 84/78.
13. Ac Bd 84/146; Govs min 84/54; Ac Bd 84/78.2; 84/102; Govs min 84/118; Ac Bd 84/97/6; Govs mins 84/29; 84/50; 84/100; Ac Bd 84/68.
14. Govs mins 84/160; 84/31; 84/51; Ac Bd 86/89.4; 87/74.2, etc; Govs mins 81/2; 81/13, 17; 81/40; KMC min 610, 24 March 1981; min 34(a), 2 June 1981; *HDE*, 9 March 1981.
15. *Report of the Committee of Enquiry into the Academic Validation of Degree Courses in Public Sector Higher Education* (The Lindop Report). Cmnd. 9501. HMSO, 1985. Ac Bd 85/4; 85/25; 85/8.1; 85/37; Govs min 85/61; Ac Bd 85/20; 85/69; 85/82, 89; Govs mins 85/16; 85/25; 85/47(i); 85/73; Ac Bd 85/39; Govs mins 85/98; 85/99. *Higher Education into the 1990s*, Cmnd. 8524. HMSO, 1985.
16. Ac Bd 85/72; 85/26.3; 85/14.2; Govs min 85/55; Ac Bd 85/72, Appendix; Govs min 85/115; Ac Bd 85/27. 'Academic Board Consultative Report. Review of the Development and Position of the Institution and Consideration of Future Policy and Organisation by Professor K J Durrands, Rector, Huddersfield Polytechnic, September/October 1985'.
17. Ac Bd 85/24; 85/34.3; Govs min 85/43; Ac Bd 85/22.1; Govs mins 85/47(v); 85/69; 85/96. The Home Secretary in March 1985 was Leon Brittan. The political context of this episode was the defeat of the miners by Mrs Thatcher's government in 1984-5.
18. Govs mins 85/111, 114; Ac Bd 85/79.2; 85/81; Govs min 85/127.
19. Govs mins 85/66, 67; Ac Bd 85/49; Govs mins 85/80; 85/17, 18; 85/53; 85/124; 85/47(iv); 85/76 and appendix; Ac Bd 85/68; Govs min 85/116.
20. Ac Bd 85/16; Govs mins 85/63; 85/106; Ac Bd 87/47.4; 85/85.
21. Govs mins 85/50; 85/79; Ac Bd 85/56; Govs mins 85/102, 104, 112.
22. Govs mins 86/30; 86/51; Ac Bd 86/21.1; 86/2.3; Govs mins 86/38; 86/20; 86/36; Ac Bd 86/61.1; 86/84.1.
23. Ac Bd 86/19, 24.3; 86/3; Govs mins 86/34; 86/118; 86/148; Ac Bd 86/18; Govs mins 86/44; 86/101, 108; Ac Bd 86/6; Govs min 86/49; 87/39(b).
24. Govs min 86/24; Ac Bd 86/2; Govs min 85/108; Ac Bd 85/68.3; 85/79.2; Govs min 86/24; Ac Bd 86/2; Govs min 86/135; Ac Bd 86/15; Govs min 86/55; Ac Bd 86/29.2; Govs min 86/70; Ac Bd 86/41.
25. Govs min 86/70; Ac Bd 86/41; Govs min 86/95; Ac Bd 86/56.1; 86/68.2; Govs mins 86/114; 86/144.
26. Govs min 86/9; Ac Bd 86/2; 86/29.3; 86/75; Govs min 86/97; Ac Bd 86/68; Govs mins 86/116; 86/146; 86/152; Ac Bd 86/89; Govs mins 86/126; 86/150; 87/6; 86/93; 86/82.

27. Govs min 86/46; Ac Bd 86/16; Govs min 86/80; Ac Bd 86/57.1; Govs min 86/127; Ac Bd 86/78.1; Govs min 86/151; Ac Bd 86/127; Ac Bd 86/78.1; Govs min 86/151; Ac Bd 86/71.2; 86/79.3; 86/67; Govs min 86/140.
28. Govs min 86/156; Ac Bd 86/89.3.
29. Govs mins 86/88, 89; 86/90; Ac Bd 86/9; Govs mins 86/65; 86/25.
30. Ac Bd 86/27; Govs min 86/62; Ac Bd 86/54; 86/60; 86/34.
31. Govs mins 86/5; 86/31; 86/119; 86/7; 86/32; 86/53; Ac Bd 86/35; Govs mins 86/98; 86/117; 86/147. There had been relief to the chronic accommodation shortage on the Queensgate campus during 1982, when the 'Firth Street Building' came into use, to house the Business Faculty. It was officially opened in May 1983 by the then Sir Harold Wilson, KG, MP, PC, a native of Huddersfield.
32. Govs min 86/168; Ac Bd 86/89; 87/3; Govs min 87/52; Ac Bd 87/54; 87/18.3.
33. Ac Bd 87/27; Govs min 87/65; Ac Bd 87/38, 31; Govs mins 87/86; 87/121; 87/157; 87/59; 87/119; Ac Bd 87/54.3; 87/61; 87/67; 87/77 *Higher Education: Meeting the Challenge* Cmd. 114. HMSO, 1987
34. Ac Bd 87/19; 87/45; Govs min 87/138; Ac Bd 87/60; Govs min 87/166; Ac Bd 87/77.
35. Govs min 87/39(b); Ac Bd 87/44.5; Govs mins 87/103; 87/19; 87/20, 23.1; Ac Bd 87/12.5; Govs mins 87/104, 107, 112; 87/127, 133; 87/159; 87/134; 87/13.
36. Ac Bd 87/32; 87/43.1; 87/32.1; 87/44.1.
37. Govs mins 87/2; 87//32; 87/36; Ac Bd 87/51; Govs mins 87/137; 87/161.
38. Govs mins 87/6; 'The Polytechnic of Huddersfield. Annual Report' (AR), 1990-1991, 6; Ac Bd 87/74 (84).
39. Govs mins 87/27; 87/26; 87/21, 22; 87/25; Polytechnic of Huddersfield Higher Education Corporation (HEC), Governing Council (GC), 98/77; 89/39.2.
40. Ac Bd 87/13.1; Govs mins 87/140, 141; Ac Bd 87/113/2; Govs min 87/50; Ac Bd 87/31; 87/68; Govs min 87/142.
41. Ac Bd 87/5; Govs min 87/69; Ac Bd 87/32.4; 87/66; 87/63(73).4; Govs mins 87/129; 87/11 - 87/14; 87/128; 87/160.4; Ac Bd 87/74(84).3,4.
42. Govs min 88/10; Ac Bd 88/9; 88/59; 88/21.1; Govs mins 88/87; 88/43, 47; 88/84, 93; Ac Bd 88/75; 88/84.
43. Polytechnic of Huddersfield HEC. Minutes of the Governing Council (GC) GC/88/1; Ac Bd 88/47.5; GC/88/9; 88/7; 89/28.
44. GC/88/3-7; 88/12; 89/7; 89/24; 89/58; Ac Bd 88/54; 89/6.2; GC/89/80; Ac Bd 89/25.1.
45. GC/88/13; 89/8; 89/20, 21; 88/15, AOBb.
46. GC/89/89; 89/112; 89/117; 89/136; 90/06; 91/32.
47. GC/89/2, 3; 89/42, 51; 89/6; 89/35; 89/31; Ac Bd 89/2.
48. GC/89/22, 25; 89/29, 37, 40, 41; 89/55, 59; 89/15.
49. Ac Bd 88/23; Govs mins 88/54, 67; 88/78.1, 2; Ac Bd 88/48.1; 88/55.1.
50. Ac Bd 88/7.1, 2; 88/87; 89/2, 4; 89/17.
51. Govs min 88/11; Ac Bd 88/10; Govs min 88/34; Ac Bd 88/18; Govs min 88/58; Ac Bd 88/75.1. 'Huddersfield Polytechnic. Institutional Review Report, January 1988'; Letter to Staff from the Rector, 7 March 1988.
52. Ac Bd 87/18.3; 87/158, 163; 88/5.2; 88/48.2; 88/66.1; 88/59; 89/18.3; 89/62; 90/2.1.
53. Govs min 88/4; Ac Bd 88/5.1; Govs mins 88/24; 88/50.
54. Govs mins 88/16; 88/91; 88/7; GC/89/13; Ac Bd 89/8; 89/12.3; Govs mins 89/56, 55.
55. Govs mins 88/12; 88/27; 88/59; 89/40; 88/82, 81; 89/3; 89/23; Ac Bd 89/16.
56. Govs mins 88/17; Ac Bd 88/17; 88/25; GC/89/25.
57. I am indebted to the late Mr T J Gaskell, formerly Pro Rector, and the late Mr M E Bond, formerly Academic Registrar, for these figures.

CHAPTER 9

IX. Coat of Arms of the Polytechnic

CHAPTER 9

THE HIGHER EDUCATION CORPORATION: POLYTECHNIC TO UNIVERSITY, 1989-92

(a) The Establishment of the Corporation, 1989-91

'The appointment of Professor Colin Adamson as "nominee" governor ... completed the initial membership of the Corporation', the Rector told Academic Board in February 1989. Of the 15 members of the new Governing Council, nine were 'independent', and were 'the Corporation'. One of them, the 'absent governor', Mrs Hill, agreed to resign in March 1990, and was replaced by Mr Albert Arnison, the now-retired 'College HMI' who had been involved in the vitally-important visit of Chief HMI Norris and others in October 1981. This adjustment occasioned 'a determination of membership numbers', which could have totalled 24. Lack of Academic Board representation was 'noted', but the existing composition confirmed. Thus, the Rector had a built-in majority of reliable supporters over the five staff, student and Local Authority representatives, whose 'appointment' had in each case to be 'referred to the independent members for recommendation' to Council membership.[1]

Mr Arnison was quickly appointed to the now-named General Purposes Committee (GPC), on which he joined its Chairman, Mr Fielden, Professor Adamson-Macedo, Mr Cross and the Rector. This Committee's first terms of reference, in July 1989, were 'to determine finance, employment and other matters ... not to be delegated ... to another committee; to advise on all matters; to deal with all matters on or moving towards the agenda of the Governing Council ...' From July 1990, '... all financial forecasts (were to) be referred to the GPC prior to promulgation ...'; and in November 1991 'estate and property matters' were added to its remit. At almost all of the Council meetings, Mr Fielden - or, in his occasional absence, Professor Adamson-Macedo or Mr Arnison - gave oral presentations of items of business considered that morning and/or on the previous day by the GPC. These were then the Council's agenda.[2]

During 1990 Mr Cross received the OBE and was made a Fellow of the Polytechnic; but there were occasional signs of his unease as President. In September he disagreed with the Rector and Mr Fielden about a 'Polytechnic Chairmen's Group', for which he was enthusiastic but which they thought inappropriate 'in the new competitive climate'. The Council supported the President on this. It had also, in 1989, supported the idea of 'The Society', with which Mr Cross was not associated. This idea was promoted by the Rector and Professor Adamson-Macedo, to 'strengthen present development and explore the Polytechnic's latent potential'; but its intended inaugural meeting, with visiting speaker, never took place. The Professor successfully campaigned nationally, however, against an attempt by the 'Polytechnics and Colleges Employers' Forum' (PCEF) - whose management board Mr Cross was to join in 1992 - to alter the lecturers' salary structure. The Polytechnic was a member of the PCEF, since it negotiated salaries, and the Council 're-affirmed' its recognition of trade unions, 'in line within the PCEF agreement'. But the Rector's uninhibited comments to Academic Board, after pay rises in 1989 and 1990, of 8 per cent and 9.6 per cent, and about strikes by 73 lecturers against the application of

82. Mr Reg Cross, OBE

new scales, were not best calculated to please Mr Cross, a life-long trade unionist. Professor Durrands commented that the pay settlements increased 'the proportion of the Polytechnic's budget ... being taken up by salaries and wages', and meant 'further erosion of other areas of expenditure'.³

The Academic Board was more subordinated to and distant from the Corporation's Governing Council than it had been in relation to the Governors of the Local Authority's Polytechnic. It had no representation on the Council, and could only set up committees with the Council's approval. The 'Strategic' or 'Corporate Plan' required by the PCFC was drawn up under the direction of the Corporation's 'statutory auditors'. The Board 'advised' on and 'endorsed' its 'final form' in July 1989. It did hold its ground on the power to make honorary awards: the Rector and Council had finally to acknowledge the Board's sole authority to make decisions on 'academic qualifications and academic distinctions'.⁴

The transition to Corporation status was accompanied by a re-organisation of the Rectorate. The General Purposes Committee was concerned 'at the heavy workload' and was intent on strengthening the senior-management team. This was done by promoting Professor Barr to be Deputy Rector and creating an additional Assistant Rectorship for Academic Affairs. This was filled internally by Dr D A Kirby, then Acting Dean of the Arts Faculty. Mr David Lock, an external appointee, was made 'Head of Secretariat and Administration' and soon also 'Secretary to the Corporation'. 'Senior management' now consisted of Rector, Deputy Rector, Pro Rector Mr Gaskell, Dr P F Arthur and Dr Kirby as Assistant Rectors, and the Secretary. Documents transferring 'assets and liabilities' from Kirklees to the Corporation were signed in January 1990, when the Governing Council was told that, despite its vociferously-expressed 'concern' about Kirklees delays, 'the Polytechnic of Huddersfield was one of the first to reach this stage'.⁵

The new Funding Council (PCFC) was as heavy a cross to bear as the old. Academic Board recorded its 'grave concern at the interference of the PCFC in the Polytechnic's affairs' in June 1990, and in October was told that 16 'circulars' had been received in the last six months, 'each one requiring great effort to reply to'. The Rector criticised the

83. Z Block

Funding Council for favouring 'low-cost bids', thereby, he complained, endangering the Polytechnic's 'range of academic provision'. Mr Gaskell told the Board that the Polytechnic had probably committed itself to taking more students for 1990-91 in some areas than would be funded; unlike the NAB, the PCFC funded institutions, not 'programme areas', and the 'disaggregation' was to be done internally. When the allocations were received, in January, he calculated that funding per FTE student would be 15 per cent less than in 1989-90. The budget would be 'tight', but 'the solvency of the Higher Education Corporation would be secured by it'. Income was estimated at £30.5m and expenditure about £29.5m.[6] The PCFC seemed to cause problems even when it was being benevolent. The vigorously opposed student loans were introduced from 1990. Accompanying their introduction, the PCFC allocated 'Access Funds', which, like loans, colleges were to administer. Huddersfield's share was £129,000. By January 1991, only one-fifth of this had been distributed, and the Board's Welfare Committee asked that the Rector withdraw his requirement that only students who had applied for loans could benefit. The Rector insisted on the condition, presumably justifiably, since the whole fund was disbursed within the session.[7]

In the colder financial climate, the Polytechnic had to generate extra income. After rejections, its bid for funding from the Training Agency, under its 'Enterprise in Higher Education' scheme, was approved for funding from January 1991. This was a five-year contract, worth over £2m, designed 'to enhance the enterprise skills of students'. It was to be described in the annual report for 1990-91 as 'the most significant feature of the year' among academic developments. Agency funding was also won for full-time courses in computing for HNC and MSc qualifications. Dr Arthur had presented a second review inside four months of 'the Polytechnic's business and industry support-service activities' in May 1989, but to a sceptical reception: the Council asked for a 'cost-benefit analysis

84. Music Block

of potential risks'. Even so, 'Huddersfield Polytechnic Enterprises Ltd' had been hopefully established. In late 1990 there were successes in contrasting academic areas in attracting funding for appointments. Brooke Crompton Hawker Siddeley gave support towards the establishment of a Chair in Power Engineering; and a shared appointment in Japanese with Sheffield University was supported by the Daiwa Anglo-Japanese Foundation.[8] Two other initiatives towards raising extra funds coalesced. In May 1989 the PCFC had made a grant of £28,000 to stimulate fund-raising. An 'Appeals Fund Committee' had been set up to formulate a 'strategic plan' 'to maximise earnings of the institution'. It became associated with the celebration of the institution's 150th anniversary, in 1991. Suggestions included the establishment of 'a chair in emerging technologies' and of 'foundation scholarships', but, since there was 'little time for a major appeal', by October 1990, the Secretary had devised a less-ambitious programme.[9]

A new academic organisation was instituted for the Polytechnic's new era. Applying the new Articles of Government, the Council asked Academic Board to 'consider' its own 're-constitution'. The Board duly endorsed a composition for its successor to conform with the Rector's academic re-organisation of the Polytechnic. He had changed the system of 20 Departments, grouped into five Faculties, into nine Schools, each under a Dean. The newly-constituted Academic Board, duly approved by the Council, held its first meeting on 27 October 1989. Its proposed committee structure also had to be approved. In this process, the Rector objected to a proposed 'Community Services Committee', and its former name, 'Welfare Committee', was restored. The most important change in the structure, completed by January 1990, was the abolition of a separate Finance Committee, which Mr Gaskell had chaired. On the Rector's

85. Great Hall and St Paul's

'recommendation', Professor Barr became Chairman of 'Academic Planning and Resources', and Dr Kirby of 'Academic Standards'.[10]

The PCFC had been given a wider remit than that of its predecessor, the NAB: it included assessment of 'quality'. In March 1990, after a scrutiny exercise, it rated three areas of the Polytechnic's work 'of exceptional (*sic*) high quality', which, the Governing Council was told, was an 'average number'. The Council resolved '... to identify measures ... to lift this Polytechnic above the average ...', and in May Academic Board approved Dr Kirby's paper on 'academic planning and academic quality'. This provided for a 'stronger annual monitoring process' and an internal 'system of academic audit ... which would include course delivery'. The Funding Council's academic-quality functions obviously undermined the position of the CNAA as the national guardian of higher-education standards outside the universities. In June, the DES decreed that institutions which had achieved full CNAA 'accreditation' - for both taught courses and research degrees - should be independent of the CNAA. Twelve polytechnics qualified. Huddersfield was 'accredited' for taught courses, and had recently received 'extended powers' in relation to its research degrees. A declared aim to achieve full research-degrees accreditation by March 1991 was not fulfilled, but in November this was granted, with effect from 1 January 1992. After the publication of Kenneth Clarke's 1991 White Paper on higher education, it was clear that the CNAA would be abolished, and likely also that the PCFC would be replaced.[11]

The Polytechnic's academic re-organisation had itself been shaped to its academic plan. The new Schools faced in a novel form the problem of how subjects should be taught (or, in the jargon, 'how the curriculum should be delivered'). This was the problem set by

86. Sports Hall

Credit Accumulation and Transfer (CAT). The group set up in December 1988 to investigate the feasibility of instituting 'a tariff system across the Polytechnic' so as to offer 'combined studies' degrees had recommended, in May 1989, that there should first be a pilot study. This began in September 1990. In December, Academic Board decided it must introduce 'a semester system for the delivery and assessment of modules'. 'Academic programmes' 'were to move, on a rolling basis, to a semester system as Credit Accumulation and Transfer is phased in'. Compatibility of course organisation across the Polytechnic was a pre-condition for 'The Polytechnic of Huddersfield Academic Credit Scheme' ('PHACS'). The *Annual Report* for 1990-91 was confident that PHACS would 'give students a greater choice in course content, allied to more flexible modes of learning'. Surprisingly, considering the relative numbers of students involved, it gave as a main justification for this drastic organisational change that it would 'be of particular benefit to part-time students', since it would 'link in-company staff-development schemes with in-service training, based at the Polytechnic.' [12]

This published report spoke of the expansion of student numbers continuing 'unabated', 'to reach a new record total of 8,758, 7 per cent above last year's figure'. That was the 'head count', not distinguishing among 'modes of learning' or levels of work: the full-time-equivalent number on higher-education courses was 6,550, which was 300 more than in 1989-90. Nor, in the process of recruitment, had a rise in numbers seemed assured. The Rector's concern about the Polytechnic's ability to maintain a 'broad spread of disciplines' and 'range of academic provision' was still justified. Dr Kirby had reported in December that 'the Polytechnic's rate of increase in enrolments in September 1990 was lower than that achieved in most Polytechnics. In particular, performance in respect of part-time students was very poor'. He was 'concerned' 'that the 11 per cent increase in applications reported nationally … is not reflected here'. In March 1991 Mr

87. Catering Annexe Building

Gaskell hoped that 'updated figures about recruitment' in Engineering 'would persuade the PCFC not to withhold funds for under-recruitment'. Necessarily, 'widening access to higher education (was) a major commitment of the Polytechnic'. After some hesitation, it had joined a West Riding consortium, in October 1989, and in May 1990 a 'policy statement' required all courses to 'set targets for admission of non-standard entries', and to adjust 'the nature of the curriculum and its delivery' to 'non-standard entrants' if necessary.[13]

Other non-standard entrants were overseas students, among whom new sources of recruitment were developed. A three-year contract, bringing 60 Malaysian students a year, had been signed in September 1989, when the first Indonesians graduated. As annual reports explained, the Polytechnic's links overseas were not confined to student recruitment. The Centre for International Education (later called 'International Office') had 'links with institutions in the West Indies, South America, Africa, the Middle East, the Far East, Eastern Europe and the EC'. There were reported to be contacts in Hungary, Poland and the Soviet Union, all of these with the School of Education, which 'attracted students from 16 countries'. 'Overseas students from across the world' were recruited to 'the Polytechnic's other courses', and it was hoped in June 1991 that students from EC countries, taking 'part-courses' and financed from a fund administered by the British Council, would increase the number.[14]

The 'delay in re-housing the Student's Union' was conveniently blamed on Kirklees Council, and 'progress had been further frustrated because the safety of the (Great Hall) building was in question'. The Rector, not satisfied with assurances given by Kirklees Technical Services, had asked consultant engineers to carry out a survey. That might 'indicate unsuitability, or that costs would be exorbitant and we do not have the money', he warned. After being closed for two terms, the building was declared fit for use in March 1990, and the Union re-occupied it in its still-unconverted state.[15] Nursery care for students' children was also being provided, until the Polytechnic's own premises were ready in early 1990, in a private nursery. In July the Council declared itself 'encouraged' by the extent of the new nursery's use, but 'concerned' at the high capital cost (£54,000), and that 'the cost per place exceeded the fee income per student'. It was accepted, though, that the nursery was 'necessary for the future of the institution', and the Secretary had secured assurance that it was legitimate to use PCFC money to subsidise it.[16]

A bigger Students' Union issue had arisen in March 1990, when a deficit of £63,000 was revealed in Union finances for 1988-89. The President-elect was asked to account for this, and in doing so revealed that the Union had formed a trading company, 'limited by shares'. She was required to furnish accounts to the Council and advised to seek legal guidance. But legal advice given later to the Corporation was that it should not regard itself as 'a shadow director of Huddersfield Polytechnic Student Services Ltd', and 'should not give advice' to it. The now-President also learned from 'legal advice', and in November demanded 'unconditional release' of the annual block grant due to the Union from the Corporation. Eventually the Corporation had to concede this. But the President punched her full weight: in January 1991 she demanded 're-imbursement for loss of bank interest while release of the block grant was suspended'. The Council appointed a negotiating group, and sparring continued till the President's last Council meeting, in June 1991. She then protested at having been excluded from the meeting of the General Purposes Committee on the previous day, when it had been decided to 're-locate' the Union in St Peter's Building, half-a-mile from the campus, and to give 'the Rector and Chairman (Mr Fielden) … powers to act on the St Peter's proposals'. The Council 'referred back' these proposals of the GPC, despite being 'advised that this decision

88. St Paul's Hall and the 1940 building: a view across the Queensgate ring road

89. The ubiquitous Castle Hill

could well place the entire accommodation strategy, strategic plan and financial plan (of the Polytechnic) in jeopardy'. There was a further Council meeting in July, whose main business was to 'appoint' the new student President and consider Union affairs. The Rector had called in 'the Corporation's external auditors' to review the Union's accounts. Lord Gregson announced that 'he had received information which indicated a possible *prima facie* case of misuse of public funds'. Mr Arnison and Professor Adamson-Macedo spoke in similar terms. Union finances were now to be examined by the Council's Audit Committee. The rest of this meeting's business was scarcely less surprising. Mr Fielden announced his 'pleasure that the Students' Union was to relocate in premises adjacent to the Queensgate campus'. The 'premises' were the Sunday School building of the former Milton Congregational Church, which, as 'Milton Hall', had been used over many years for music teaching. Finally the external auditor was asked whether, 'having heard the discussion of the possible misuse of funds', he was 'willing to sign … the audit report'. He 'replied that he was happy to sign'.[17]

The Polytechnic's own finances were evidently well-conducted and healthy. At the end of the first financial year, in March 1990, there was a 'reserve figure of £2.4m', and the Council was later told that Huddersfield had the fourth largest surplus that year among 24 polytechnics surveyed. Estimated income for 1990-91 was £33.3m and for 1991-2 £37.848m, but the bids to the PCFC for the student numbers to give this income would raise the student/staff ratio to 15:1. The Polytechnic had to live within the means it had claimed it could in its strategic plan. A revised plan, covering 1991-5, was designed to

90. 1883 building: a view across the Queensgate ring road

maintain the existing range of work. To do that was 'expensive', the Rector warned, and it would be 'necessary to change the balance in student numbers' towards courses that were cheaper to run; and all was based on the assumption that PCFC funding would move towards the higher levels of the Universities Funding Council (UFC). This was looking to the ending of 'the binary line', a possibility first mentioned in March 1991.[18]

Expanding numbers made more acute the accommodation problems, teaching and residential. PCFC money could not be spent on providing student accommodation, and Huddersfield owned the lowest number of residential places among the polytechnics. Over £1m received from the PCFC was spent repairing teaching accommodation in 1989-90, but the pressing need was 'to extend the Queensgate campus', as the Rector told Academic Board in October 1990. The best way to do this was to acquire more mill buildings on Firth Street, where Larchfield had already been converted. In July 1990 the Council was told about approaches being made to purchase 'Lawton's Mill', a huge complex contiguous with the campus; but in May 1991 it was announced that 'the polytechnic had not been successful in its bid ...', and the Council was persuaded to 'approve the purchase of residential accommodation on this site ... from Court (Warwickshire) Ltd. for a sum close to £6.2m for September 1992'. Comparably significant was an earlier report, in March, in the *Huddersfield Examiner*, of an offer by 'a local benefactor to make a substantial contribution to the cost of purchasing the Storthes Hall Estate', the 470-acre site of a former mental hospital four miles from the Polytechnic. Academic Board, having heard the Rector's explanation of the story, 'recognised the considerable potential ...' of the property and 'asked that the benefactor, who wished to remain anonymous, be personally advised of the Board's gratitude'. This was the 'accommodation strategy' that, it was alleged, would be put 'in jeopardy' by the Student President's victory at the June council meeting. Her triumph did not prevent the document from being discussed with the PCFC in July.[19]

At the end of two academic years, in the summer of 1991 the Polytechnic had changed in many ways by its being a Higher Education Corporation. The Corporation entered into contracts with the Funding Council, and it did so with staff. Salaries and conditions of service were still nationally negotiated for grades up to Principal Lecturer; above that, there were individual contracts, and a new status, of Professors whose posts were 'linked to contracts of employment and subjects', was introduced. The Rectorate was again re-organised in 1991. Mr Gaskell retired in March, with the Rector's thanks for his 'enormous contribution' over 17 years. Two new Assistant Rectors were appointed, so that the Rectorate of 1991-2 consisted of Rector, Deputy Rector and four Assistant Rectors: Dr P F Arthur and Dr Kirby; and Professor Fen Arthur who came from

91. A view of the Polytechnic

Birmingham Polytechnic, and Dr W J Rea, who had been an HMI.[20]

The structure of higher education was to be changed by the issue of the White Paper, *Higher Education: A New Framework*, by the Secretary of State, Kenneth Clarke, in May 1991. He made three main proposals: to allow polytechnics to change their names to universities; to allow them to award their own degrees; and to merge the higher-education Funding Councils (PCFC and UFC). Professor Durrands thought the first proposal 'the most important', because 'it would allow the Polytechnic to compete more equally in the market and help to break down the so-called academic and vocational barrier'. He asked the Board 'to give thought to the title, bearing in mind the service given to Calderdale'. 'University of West Yorkshire and University of the West Riding have been mentioned' he told it. The Board wanted 'Huddersfield', but the Rector persisted till December, when the Secretary reported that 'the replies received in the consultation exercise ... had shown a large majority in favour of 'The University of Huddersfield' '.[21]

(b) 'A Happy and Successful Year', 1991-92

In his 'President's Foreword' to 'the last report of the former Polytechnic', which covered the period 1 April 1991 to 31 March 1992, Mr Cross described 'the past year' as 'a happy and successful one which signalled a watershed in British Higher Education'. The Polytechnic celebrated its 150th anniversary, and 'the celebrations (would) continue into next year as the Polytechnic marks its designation as a University'. The year marked a 'watershed' because 'the Further and Higher Education Act 1992 gave public recognition to the sound achievements of the polytechnic sector over the last 21 years'. The Rector picked out as 'the most striking change over 1991-92' 'the significant increase in enrolments - full-time students up by 23 per cent, sandwich students up by eight per cent and part-time students by 17 per cent'. 'As a consequence of the ... 1992 Act, the higher education branch of the Inspectorate, the Council for National Academic Awards (CNAA) and the Polytechnics and Colleges Funding Council (PCFC) will be wound up ...' He thanked them all, valedictorily, for having 'provided help and encouragement to the maintenance of standards and the development of the curriculum'. Students completing courses that session would be the last to receive CNAA degrees: from September 1992, institutions like Huddersfield would award their own.[22]

In February 1992 the Governing Council had been told that 'the recommended request to

92. Huddersfield roofscape

the Privy Council for the Institution to be known as 'The University of Huddersfield' had been submitted', and the name was promulgated in the *London Gazette* on 8 May. On 'the recommendation of the General Purposes Committee', the Council adopted the title for Professor Durrands of 'Vice-Chancellor and Principal', 'with immediate effect' on 22 May. Told of the Privy Council's formal consent, on 16 June, to the name 'The University of Huddersfield', and to its authorisation to confer degrees, the Council, again prompted by the GPC, resolved 'that the words "Higher Education Corporation" should only be added to the name of the University where the addition is required by law'. It authorised the Rector to acquire a new mace, declining an offer of the former Huddersfield Corporation's mace. Its proposal 'that the celebration should include a church service' was, however, rejected by the Academic Board.[23] The first meeting of the University Council, in July, was itself celebratory. 'Great pleasure' was recorded at the award in the Queen's Birthday Honours list of the CBE to Professor Durrands, 'Vice-Chancellor and Rector'. Mr Cross was made first Chancellor of the University, 'until a new Instrument and Articles of Government are made or until the 1993 Annual General Meeting, whichever is the sooner'. Professor Durrands summarised 'national developments arising from the removal of the binary line': the merging of the Committee of Directors of Polytechnics into the Committee of Vice-Chancellors and Principals (CVCP) and of the two admissions systems ('PCAS' and 'UCCA'); and co-operation between - but not yet merging of - the two Funding Councils (PCFC and UFC). At the AGM which followed, Mr Cross and Mrs Carter were re-elected President and Vice-President of the Council, and three retiring Independent Members were re-elected by their fellows.[24]

The academic year 1991-2 was a particularly successful one for Professor Durrands, and one in which the corporation entered into a new 'service contract' with him. He suffered a disappointment, however, when a proposal by the General Purposes Committee, in February 1992, that the Central Services Building be re-named 'the Durrands Building' was 'referred back' by the Council. At its next meeting the Council resolved that 'for the present' there be 'no further consideration given to the names of buildings'. For Professor Barr, 1992 was a doubly notable year. The Council was told in February that he would be retiring on 31 March, and passed a vote of thanks. It then received a paper explaining that Professor Adamson-Macedo's period of appointment as 'additional nominee' member had expired on 25 January, and the Secretary 'had received a nomination for

93. An academic procession

Professor Barr to be appointed …' Despite an objection, he was confirmed as 'Additional Nominee of the Corporation' at the May meeting of Council, when he was, at its recommendation, also appointed a member of the GPC. He did not attend his first meetings until the autumn term, when, in Mr Fielden's absence, he was Acting Chairman of the first General Purposes Committee meeting he attended.[25]

For polytechnic staff, teaching assessment by HM Inspectors was being replaced by 'quality assessment' by the Funding Council. University teachers had never been assessed; now there was to be one system. In January 1992 Academic Board was told of 'a joint exercise in quality assessment conducted in institutions across the binary line'. There was a protracted controversy about 'observation of classroom teaching to appraise staff', a development the unions opposed. In the end, the Board accepted the validity of observation of teaching 'in support of the maintenance of academic standards', but not 'in the context of national pay agreements'. It 'noted the continuing scepticism across the (higher-education) sector about the link between assessment of quality and levels of funding', which it shared. The Rector tried to re-assure members by reporting talks among Vice-Chancellors and ex-Directors on their respective 'quality audit' and 'quality assessment' units.[26]

The ultimate purpose of teaching-quality measurement was to maintain or raise the standards of students. Dr Kirby had often made that connection, and also pointed out that Huddersfield had 'a significantly lower proportion of first class honours degrees than the CNAA system as a whole'. 'While the institution's proportion of good honours-degree awards had risen steadily over the last ten years or so, the proportion of firsts had remained the same'. He urged Deans 'to ask Boards of Examiners to carefully examine their practices and to be mindful of the influence that tradition can exercise …' He returned to the theme at the Board's meeting on the eve of examinations, in May. When the Council, at its special request, was given details of honours classifications in the November 1992 awards ceremonies, it recorded its 'pleasure at the number of first-class honours' awarded.[27]

Student recruitment in 1991-2 was 'to target' in all programme areas but one, and little below in that. 'The Polytechnic exceeded its PCFC contract and enrolled a record 10,151 students in all categories - a 16% increase on the previous year.' Forty additional academic appointments were made, but the student/staff ratio was 14.85:1, compared with 14:1 the year before. The percentage increase in student numbers was by far the highest in the institution's history. It was a year, though, in which student affairs were much less prominent on the Council's agenda. Union finances improved, to the 'cautious satisfaction' of the Chairman of the Audit Committee. Normal courtesies were restored: the retiring Union President was thanked at the May 1992 Council meeting, 'especially for the improvement in financial management'.[28]

There was much activity on the property front. Professor Arthur, whose responsibilities included resources, told Academic Board in January 1992 that, 'subject to the availability of funds', the Polytechnic intended to develop Lawton's Mill for use by the School of Computing and Mathematics. Council resolved 'to proceed with the proposal to develop Canalside West Mill', the name by which this western end of the complex would henceforth be known. Nothing was said about 'Court (Warwickshire) Ltd'. It was Storthes Hall that attracted most attention. In special meetings in April, it was decided to 'make a formal application to the PCFC to be allowed to proceed to the purchase ...' In the Rector's view, there would be 'financial problems for the first five years', but then '... enormous benefit to the institution'. Professor Arthur explained that Storthes Hall could be developed 'to provide 1,600 student residences and an additional 32,500m^2 of teaching space at roughly half the cost of a new building'. Academic Board and Council members gave their support and the move to purchase went ahead. There was still talk about 'a potential benefactor', but at the end of the academic year the prospects were less clear. Professor Arthur explained in May that 'in view of the application of space norms the Institution was unlikely to receive financial assistance for this development, although indicative approval had been granted to proceed'. In July, the new University's 'Vice-Chancellor and Rector' told the Board that 'there was some doubt as to who held clear title to the property', but the University had made an offer for the whole complex 'to the receivers'. A grant from the Wolfson Foundation towards the cost of re-furbishing 'Z Block', the 1960s building, must have seemed a simple and welcome transaction in comparison.[29]

94. University Central Services Building. An artist's impression.

Notes on Chapter 9

[1] Ac Bd 89/6; 3rd meeting of GC, 17 February 1989; GC/90/27; 90/56; 90/73; 90/72; 89/158; 90/99, 100; 90/124; 91/1; 90/114; 91/79; 91/80.

[2] GC/90/130; 91/10; 90/115; 89/102; 90/75; 91/71; 13th meeting of GC, 21 September 1990.

[3] GC 16 November 1990; GC/91.1; Ac Bd 90/18.1; GC/90/71; 90/95; 90/107; 89/96.5; 89/115; 89/94; 89/121; 92/13; 92/52; 89/97; 89/125; 90/130; 89/132; 90/132; 90/57.4; 90/68.2; 91/34.

[4] GC/89/74; 89/73a; Ac Bd 89/29.1; 89/45; GC 89/103; Ac Bd 89/40, Extra-ord. meeting, 19 June 1989; Ac Bd 89/66, Extra-ord. meeting, 10 November 1989; GC/89/145; 90/12, 13; Ac Bd 90/7.4; GC/90/48; GC/37; GC/52; 90/31; Ac Bd 90/33; GC/90/93.

[5] GC/89/73(a); Ac Bd 89/28.2; GC/89/107; 89/134; 89/133; 89/137; 89/149; 90/06; 89/140, 141; 90/22.

[6] Ac Bd 90/36.2; 90/51.2; GC/90/31; Ac Bd 90/27.2; GC/89/69; 89/101; Ac Bd 89/60, 61; 89/69.1; GC/90/06; Ac Bd 90/17.2; GC/90/34, 36; Ac Bd 90/3.1; 8(b), (c); 90/17.3; GC/90/34.

[7] GC/90/116; Ac Bd 90/56.2; GC/90/130; GC/91/10; Ac Bd 91/14.2; 89/65; GC/90/113; Ac Bd 91/21.2; 91/36.

[8] Ac Bd 89/25, 31; 90/20; 90/26; 90/50; 91/28; *The Polytechnic of Huddersfield, Annual Report, 1990-1991*, pp.5, 8, 18; *Enterprise in Higher Education. Information Leaflet*, January 1991; Ac Bd 90/65; 91/13; 90/53; GC/90/133; 89/81; 89/75; 90/94; 90/130; 91/14; 91/25.

[9] GC/89/78; 89/110; 89/126; 89/140, 141; 90/59, 60; 90/79; 90/06; 90/18; 90/10; 90/59.

[10] GC/89/80; Ac Bd 89/25; GC/89/73; Ac Bd 89/30; Ac Bd Extra-ord meeting, 19 June 1989; Ac Bd 89/48; GC/89/129, 131; Ac Bd 89/55; 89/58; Extra-ord meeting, 89/66, 10 November 1989; GC/89/145; Ac Bd 89/72; GC/90/12, 13; 90/37; 80/52; Ac Bd 89/66.3.

[11] Ac Bd 90/60.1, 2; GC/90/36; Ac Bd 90/28; Ac Bd 90/13; GC/90/41; Ac Bd 90/36; 90/67.3; 91/25 (b); 91/37; 91/47.1; *Higher Education: A New Framework*, HMSO, 1991.

[12] Ac Bd 89/32; 85/59; 90/5; 90/43.1; 90/71, 72; 91/25(a).2; 91/34; 91/31.2. *Annual Report, 1990-1991*, pp.8-9.

[13] Ac Bd 90/66. 1-4; 91/2; 91/12.1; 91/24; *Annual Report, 1990-1991*, p.9; Ac Bd 89/33, 34; 89/64, pp.1, 2; 90/6; 90/29; GC/91/10; Ac Bd 91/16.3; *Annual Report, 1990-1991*, p.9.

[14] GC89/116; Ac Bd 89/50.2, 3; *Annual Report, 1990-1991*, 6; Ac Bd 90/74.4; 91/38.2.

[15] GC/89/64; 89/73(b); 89/96.3; 89/100; 89/111.2; 89/112.2; 89/140; 90/05; 90/23; 89/140; 90/06.

[16] GC/90/59; 90/109; 90/130; 89/96.2; 89/124; 89/140; 90/59; 90/87; 90/106.

[17] GC/90/39; 90/59; 90/67; 90/77; 90/103; 90/121; 91/4; 90/137; 91/6; 91/10; 91/25; 91/35; General Purposes Committee (GPC) 91/40; GC/91/40, 45-47; 91/51, 52, 55, 60.

[18] GC/90/10; 90/33-41; Ac Bd 90/57; GC/90/130; 90/128; Papers for 16th Meeting of GC, 22 March 1991; GC/91/28; 91/10; Ac Bd 91/4; 3; 91/11; GPC meeting, 7 April 1991; GC/91/34.

[19] GC/89/133, 137; Ac Bd 90/561; GC/90/68; 90/87; 90/109; Ac Bd 90/57.2; GC/90/06. 0-59; 90/78; Ac Bd 90/57.2; GPC/91/46; GC/91/46; GC/91/56; Ac Bd 91/15.3; 91/29.1; GPC 91/40; Ac Bd 91/40; 91/38.3, 4; GC/91/58.

[20] GC/91/46; 91/51, 53; Ac Bd 91/47.6; GC/91/68; 91/71, 68; GC/90/38; Ac Bd 91/17; GC/91/40; 91/57; Ac Bd 91/29.2; 91/38; 91/47; GC/91/78; Ac Bd 91/15.1, 2; GC/91/25, 32; Ac Bd 91/4; GC/91/34; 91/65; 91/41.

[21] Ac Bd 91/40.1; GC/91/10; Ac Bd 85/27; 91/25(b).3; GC/91/40, 43; Ac Bd 91/40.1; GC/91/7; Ac Bd 91/55.

[22] *The University of Huddersfield (Formerly THE POLYTECHNIC). Annual Report, 1991-1992(AR)*, 1-5, 29; Ac Bd 91/44.2, 4; 91/51; 91/47.1; GC/91/73; Ac Bd 92/4; 91/47.2; 92/30.4; 92/41; 92/50; 92/68; 92/64; 92/65.1; 92/3.2; 92/63.1(ii); 92/53.2; 92/30.2; 92/30.6; 92/39.1; 92/63; GC/92/70.

[23] GC/92/17-19; Ac Bd 92/31.1; GC/92/33, 37; 92/44; 92/52.4(i); 92/55; Ac Bd 92/39.2.

[24] GC/92/45; 92/52.4(ii); 92/60; GC/AGM/92/03, 04, 05.

[25] GC/92/03, 13; 92/33; 92/04; 92/27, 33; 92/70.

[26] *AR*, 1991-1992, 24; GC/91/72; Ac Bd 92/3.1; 92/7.2; GC/92/31, 33; Ac Bd 92/37.1,2; 92/20.1; 92/40.1, 2; 92/44.1; GC/92/49.

[27] Ac Bd 92/26, 29.5; GC/92/73.

[28] Ac Bd 91/43; *AR 1991-1992*, 6; Ac Bd 92/29; GC/92/06; Ac Bd 91/56; GC/92/38; 91/70; 92/09; 92/58; 92/41.

[29] Ac Bd 92/7.3; GC/92/52.4(ii); Ac Bd 92/23; GC/93/32(a), (b); Article of Government 46; GC/92/36; Ac Bd 92/68; 92/44.2; GC/92/51; 92/41.

POSTSCRIPT

X. Architectural detail, St. Paul's

POSTSCRIPT

In his oral report on 1 June 1970, the new Director had told Governors that 'we are considered by many to be at the bottom of the Third Division' among the polytechnics. By the time of his written 'Biennial Report ...' of June 1972, he could 'confidently say we are no longer in the Third Division ...'. There are no comparative data on the 20 new polytechnics (and ten more then planned) of June 1970. In his speech at the 1977 Awards Ceremony, Mr Durrands recalled the 1970 judgement, and attributed it to 'the then Chief Officer of the CNAA' (Mr F R Hornby). He told his 1977 audience that he 'was greatly encouraged' when he heard it, 'in April 1970', and added, 'I think it is now accepted nationally that we are in the first division'. Professor Durrands could claim in his 'Rector's Report' for 1989-90 that 'the Polytechnic was placed 5th out of 30 in the Times Top Table of degree performance at Polytechnics, published in October 1989'.

National circumstances dictated that the era of the Polytechnics was one of what then seemed spectacular growth for them. Huddersfield expanded commensurately with its potential: over the 15 years 1974-5 to 1990-91 there was an average annual increase in its higher-education student numbers of about four per cent, so that the '16 per cent' of 1991-2 was an explosion. The most indicative aspect of the Polytechnic's history was its changed academic profile. Over the 22 years its comprehensive character was preserved. Teaching still ranged in standard from 'Non-Advanced FE' to post-graduate research, but the variety of courses widened beyond comparison. In 1970 Mr Durrands had hoped his Governors would 'support a comprehensive policy' and 'give the same priority to sub-degree work as to degree and higher degree courses', so that the 'tradition of ... vocational education' would be preserved. There was then a tradition of research only in Chemistry, and recent developments in Electrical Engineering. In the academic year 1970-71 there were courses in Chemistry, Electrical Engineering, Engineering Systems, Textile Marketing and Music for honours degrees of the CNAA, and teaching for the external degrees of BA (London) - in English, History, Geography and French - and BEd (Leeds). Courses for or towards professional qualifications were offered in Architecture, Chemistry and Engineering, and for the Teacher's Certificate in Education. There were also Higher National and National Diploma and Certificate courses and some craft courses, many of these about to be transferred to the Technical College. The published annual report for 1991-2 still recorded 'pre-vocational' and 'vocational training', and teaching 'from Certificate to PhD level'. Of 12 courses new that year, four were post-graduate and six for first degrees or new pathways on existing degree courses; one was a certificate course, and one an in-service 'CAT' scheme for teachers. The subject range of these new courses included Business, Education, Music, Management, Humanities, Engineering Technology, Textile Technology, Podiatry and Health Care. Forty more new courses were reportedly included in the new corporate plan. That year, 'the value of research contracts in hand exceeded £4 million ... and in addition the PCFC awarded the Polytechnic £250,000 for research ...'. Teaching designed to develop students' 'personal transferable skills' - like the work experience under the 'Enterprise in Higher Education' scheme, devised to 'enhance the enterprise skills of students' - was preserving that 'tradition of vocational education' that the new Director had spoken about in 1970. As Vice-Chancellor and Rector, Professor Durrands still believed it would 'help to lay to rest

---

* In *The Times's* list of 'THE 100 TOP UK UNIVERSITIES', 27 May 2005, Huddersfield was number 72 and in the Guardian 'University Guide 2013: University League Table' was number 48.

the inappropriate distinction which is still made by some, through lack of understanding, between so called academic and vocational courses'.[2]

Notes on Postscript

[1] The Polytechnic, Huddersfield, 'Director's Report to the Governing Council, June 1970 and June 1972'; Govs min 72/63, 15 June 1972; 'Rector's 1 April 1977 Awards Ceremony Address and 7th Annual Report', Ac Bd 77/165, 21 October 1977; *The Polytechnic of Huddersfield. Annual Report 1989-1990*, p.6; *The Times*, 19 May 1995.

[2] *The University of Huddersfield (formerly The Polytechnic), Annual Report 1991/1992*, 4, 6, 14, 16, 18; 'Director's Report ... June 1972', pp.5, 9, 10-14; *The Polytechnic of Huddersfield, Annual Report 1990-91*, p.7. I am indebted for data on the period 1975-6 to 1990-91 to the late Mr T J Gaskell, formerly Pro Rector.

Appendix
Heads of the Institution 1841-1992

SECRETARIES
Mechanics' Institution

1844-1846	Robert Neil, 'Acting Secretary'
1846-1854	George Searle Phillips
1854-1862	Frank Curzon
1862-1864	W F Crook
1864-1879	Joseph Bate
1879-1882	D Sharman
1882-1894	Austin Keen, FCS

PRINCIPALS
Huddersfield Technical School & Mechanics' Institute

1894-1895   G S Turpin, MA, DSc.

Huddersfield Technical College

1896-1903   S G Rawson, DSc, FIC.
1904-1937   J F Hudson, MA, BSc.
1938-1946   J W Whitaker, BSc, PhD, FRIC, M Inst FUCL, M I Mech E.
1946-1958   W E Scott, BSc, MSc, PhD, FRIC.

Huddersfield College of Technology
1958-1970   W E Scott, MBE, BSc, MSc, PhD, FRIC.

DIRECTOR (RECTOR from 1972)

The Polytechnic of Huddersfield
1970-1992   K J Durrands, MSc, C Eng, FI Mech E, FIEE, FI Prod E.

VICE-CHANCELLOR AND RECTOR

The University of Huddersfield

1992 (-1994)   Professor K J Durrands, CBE, MSc, C Eng,
FI Mech E, FIEE, FI Prod E.

The Author

After war service in the Royal Navy (Fleet Air Arm), the author graduated and trained as a teacher at Manchester University. He was appointed Senior Lecturer in History at the then Huddersfield College of Technology in 1964, after 14 years as Head of History and Librarian at Penistone Grammar School. When the college became a Polytechnic, in 1970, he was a Principal Lecturer. He was made Head of the newly-created Department of History and Political Studies in 1972, and from 1982 was Head of the Department of Humanities and Dean of the Faculty of Arts. In 1984 he was made a professor of the Polytechnic. He retired in April 1989.

95. Professor John O'Connell

INDEX

Academic Board (Polytechnic)	Ch.6-9 *passim*	Brittan, Leon	129 n.17
Academic Plan (Polytechnic)	98	Brook Crompton Hawker Siddeley	138
Adamson, Prof. (Dr.) Colin	85, 111, 122, 123, 135, 143, 146	Brooke, John	7,13
		Brooke, Lady	43
Advanced Further Education (AFE) Pool	73, 128	Brooke, Sir John Arthur, Bart	42,43
		Brooke, Sir Thomas, Bart.	18,25,42
Albany Mills	121	Broomhead & Neals	91,92
Andersonian Institution, Glasgow	1	Brougham, Henry P., Baron	1,13
Anderton Committee	59	Burnip, Prof. M.S.	116
Appeals Fund Committee	138	Business & Technical Education Council (BTEC)	117
Armitage Charity	18		
Armstrong Dr. Stewart, Deputy Rector	74, 88	Butler, R.A.	49
Armytage Family	4	Canalside West Mill	148
Arnison, A. (HMI)	92,100,111,135, 143	Carlile, J.W.	20, n.5
		Carter. Cllr. Jane	85,88,91,92,93, 113,121,122,146
Arthur, Prof. Fenwick Assistant Rector	144, 148	CAT (Credit Accumulation and Transfer)	127,140,155
Arthur, Dr. P.F., Assistant Rector	116,120,127,136, 137,144	CATS: see Colleges of Advanced Technology	59,73
Articles of Government (also see Instrument)	99,122,123,138	Central Services Building (CSB)	75,85,146
Askwith, Baron	42	Centre for Industrial & Educational Liaison (CIEL)	120
Asquith, H.H.	50 n.8		
Association of Metropolitan Authorities (AMA)	111	Centre for International Education ("International Office")	141
Audit Committee	148	Chamber of Commerce	17,18
Audit Report	90	Chancellor (University)	146
Avery Hill Training College	48,49	Chapel (College)	62
		Charity Commissioners	18,26
Baker, Kenneth W.	117	Charles University, Prague	119
Ball, Christopher	112	Chief Administrative Officer (CAO)	101
Barlow Committee and Report	55		
Barr, Prof. Frank, Deputy Rector	77,89,90,109, 111,122,136,139, 146,147	Child, Rev. Alfred	19
		Church Institute	14
		City & Guilds of London Institute (CGLI)	15,19,43,46
Bastin, N.A.	101,122		
Bate, Joseph	16,18	Clarke, Kenneth	139,145
Beaumont, George P.	7	CNAA: see Council	
Bentley, Phyllis	47	'Cockerton judgements', 1900, 1901	26
Beveridge Report (1942)	49		
'Biennial Report …. 1970-2'	73,155	Coggan, Archbishop FDC	60
Birkbeck, George	1	College Associateship	44,45
Birkbeck College	1	Colleges of Advanced Technology (CATS)	58
Black, Prof. G.	91		
Blackwood, J.T.	73	Committee of Directors of Polytechnics	146
Blamires, Ald. Joseph	41,47		
Board of Education (1899)	26, 32,33	Committee of Vice-Chancellors and Principals (CVCP)	146
Board of Trade	6		
Board Schools	25	Computer (mainframe)	61,75,86
Bond, M.E., Registrar	73	Conlon, Lawrence	90,94
Bosley, Dr. J.	59	Contemporary Music Festival: see Huddersfield	
Bradford College of Art	77		
Bretton Hall College	86	Council for National Academic Awards	59,60,61,63,73, 79,87,88,89,92, 93,94,95,96,97, 99,107,109,111, 112,113,114,118, 126,139,145,147, 155
Brigg, John F.	7,17,19,42		
British and Foreign Society School	2,4		
British Association for the Advancement of Science	56		
British Council	114,119,141		
British Dyes Ltd.	41,42,47		

159

Countess de Gray and Ripon	14	Education Department of the Privy Council	15,16,26,
Court (Warwickshire) Ltd	144,148	Education, Faculty of	86
Crosland, Anthony	58,60	Education, School of	99
Crosland, Sir Joseph	26	'Enterprise in Higher Education'	137,155
Crosland, T.P.	20 n.5, 35 n.7	'Evening continuation schools'	26,29,31,32
Cross, R.C., OBE	91,113,121,122, 135,136,145,146	Everest, Dr. A.E.	41,42
Curzon, Frank	13,14	Faculties	73,117
Dalton, John	1	Fellowships, Polytechnic	75,114,135
Dawson, Ald. John L.	60	Fielden, P.H.	88,89,90,95, 96,99,101,107, 108,109,110,122, 123,135,142,143, 147
Day Science School	28,29,30,32		
Day Teacher Training School	29,31		
Deans of Faculties	73,117		
Deloitte, Haskins and Sells	124		
Dennell, Mary	73,74	Fine Art & Industrial Exhibition, 1883	19
Department of Education & Science (DES)	60,73,74,75,86, 90,91,92,93,95, 108,109,113,114, 115,116,117,118, 122,139	First World War	41
		Fisher, H.A.L.	41
		Fixby Hall	4
		Fowler, G.T.	74
Department of Scientific & Industrial Research (DSIR)	47	Freshers' Conference	62
		Gaskell, T.J., Pro Rector	77,85,88,95,96, 107,116,121,125, 127,136,137,138, 141,144
Department of Trade & Industry (DTI)	118,119		
Departments (College) *passim*			
Architecture		'Geddes Axe' (1922)	42,47
Art, Art & Design		General Purposes Committee	135,136,142, 146,147
Catering & Domestic Science			
Chemistry & Coal Tar Chemistry		'GERBIL' (Great Education Reform Bill' (1986)	117,121
Dyeing			
Education		Glasgow Mechanics' Institution	1
Engineering		Goderich, Viscount: see Ripon, Marquess of	
Chemical Engineering			
Electrical Engineering		Governing Body, Governors (Polytechnic)	Ch. 6-8 *passim*
Mechanical Engineering			
Humanistic Studies		Governing Council (Higher Education Corporation)	Ch.8-9 *passim*
Humanities			
Law		Graham, Sir James	4
Mathematics		Graves, A.P., HMI	17
Music		Gray, Ald. H.A. Bennie	63
Dixon, J, C.E.O. Kirklees MBC	93	Gray, Harold, CEO, Huddersfield CBC	64,77
Drayton, M.N.	96		
Driver, H.	122	Great Exhibition, 1851	15
Durrands, Prof. K.J., CBE, Rector *passim*		Great Hall	61,114,117,120, 128,141
Eastwood, Edmund	6	Green Paper on Higher Education 1985	112
Eccles, Sir David	57		
Edinburgh School of Arts	1	Greenwood, Arthur	47
Education Acts:		Gregson (Lord)	123,143
1870 (Elementary)	16		
1876	17	Haigh, N.	121
1918 ('Fisher')	47	Harding, G.C.F.	91
1936	47	Harman, Cllr. J.A.	122
1944 ('Butler')	49,92	HMI (Her Majesty's Inspectors of Schools)	16,17,33,60,86, 92,100,112,114, 135,147
1962	59		
1992 (Further & Higher)	145		
'Education Blue Book' (1882)	17		
Education Committee (Huddersfield CBC)	29	Higher Education Act, 1991	31
		Higher Education Corporation (1989)	85,137,144,146

Higher Grade School	25,26,30	Joseph, Sir Keith	115,117
Hiley, Samuel	7	Jubilee Extension	26
Hill, Mrs. K.	122,135	Junior Technical School	42
Hirst, Ald. Albert	46		
History, MA degree in	112	Kalungi, Ephraim S.	62
Hodgson, Dr. H.H.	42,63	Kaye, George, FRS	48
Holland, Ms. Ismena	7, 60,63	Keen, Austin	16,17
Holly Bank Campus	57,74,77,115,121	Kell, S.C.	3,7
		Kerr, Dr. Edwin, C.E., CNAA	94,96,97,98,101,107,126
Hong Kong	119		
Hornby, F.R.	155	Kirkby, Dr. D.A.	136,139,140,144,147
Huddersfield Banking Company	5		
Huddersfield Chronicle	13,14,16,17,25,27	Kirklees Hall	4
		Kirklees Metropolitan Borough Council (MBC)	Chapters 7-8 *passim*,136,141
Huddersfield College	Chapter 3 *passim*		
Huddersfield College of Education (Technical)	74	Chief Executive	85,99
		Education Committee	77,85,86,121
Huddersfield Collegiate School	3	Education Services, Director of	92
Huddersfield Contemporary Music Festival	112	Finance Director	88,89,90,94,95,114
Huddersfield Corporation	27	Technical Services	95,107,141
Huddersfield Corporation Act	27	Korean War (1950-3)	55
Huddersfield Corporation Bill	27		
Huddersfield County Borough Council	27,29,144	Larchfield Mills	124,127,144
		Lawton's Mill	144,148
Huddersfield (Daily) Examiner	25,89,90,144	Layfield, Sir Frank, QC	92,94,97,98,107,109,110,110n
Huddersfield Female Educational Institute	17	Lee, Dr. H.D.C.	41
		Levinstein Ltd	41
Huddersfield Mechanics' Institution	3 *passim*	Library	3,15,27,28,34,47,61,75,125
Huddersfield Philosophical Society	1		
Huddersfield Polytechnic Enterprises Ltd	138	Lindop, Sir Norman	112
		Lindop Report	112,114
Huddersfield Polytechnic Student Services Ltd.	142	Local Government Act, 1888	26
		Local Government Act, 1958	59
Huddersfield Regional College of Technology	46-52, *passim*	Local Taxation (Customs and Excise) Act, 1890	26
Huddersfield School Board	25	Lock, David	136
Huddersfield Scientific and Mechanic Institute	1, 2	*London Gazette*	146
		London Mechanics Institute	1
Huddersfield Technical College	26,28,29	London University	25,34,58,63
Huddersfield Technical School and Mechanics Institution	13,17	Lowenthal, Joseph	7
		Lunn, Edgar	63
Huddersfield Town FC	62		
Huddersfield Young Men's Mental Improvement Society	2	MacLennan, A.	77
		Magnus, Sir Philip	19
Hudson, J.F., Principal	32,44,46,47,64	Malawi Polytechnic	119
Hughes, Edward	18	Malaysian students	141
Hughes, Dr J.S.	121	Manchester University (see Victoria University)	
Huth, Edward , J.P.	7, 18		
		Manpower Service Commission (MSC)	116,117,119
Ibbotson, Derek, G.	62		
Imperial College, London	34	Marriott, William	7, 14, 18
Indonesian students	115,119,141	Mason, Cllr.	92,94
Instrument and Articles of Government	85,86,89,98,107,109,121,146	MBA degree	112
		Mellor, Wright	7
		Mernagh, Cllr. John	92,93,94,95,100,109,113
Instrument of Accreditation (CNAA)	118		
		Milton Hall	143
International Student Society	62	Miners' Welfare Fund	46
		Mock Turtle	47,62
Jarmain, George	14,15,16		
John Brooke & Sons	13,18		

National Advisory Body (NAB)	107,108,111,112, 113,114,115,118, 119,127,137,139	'Ravensknowle', Ravensknowle Park	43
		Rawson, Dr. S.G., Principal	26,28,29,31,32, 33,46,47,48,56, 64
National Association for the Promotion of Technical and Secondary Education	26	Rea, Dr. W.J.	145
National Certificates and Diplomas:		Read Holliday Ltd.	41
Ordinary (ONC, OND)	44	Rector (title)	passim
Higher (HNC, HND)	44,119,137	Regent Street Polytechnic	85
National Council for Technological Awards (NCTA)	58,59	Regional Council (for Further & Higher Education)	60
National Pooling Committee	85	Research, Dean of	116
Neil, Robert	4	Ripon, Marquess of	14,25
Nelson's Buildings, New Street	3	Robbins Report on Higher Education	59,60,61
Nettleton's Charity	18		
Newbold, Prof. David	35n	Robert, Prof. J-F.	113
Nigerian Polytechnics	119	'Roles and Relationships' (with Kirklees MBC)	85,88,89,107, 109,114,119
Norris, E. (Chief HMI)	100,135		
Nursery	120,124,128,142	Royal Commission on Technical Instruction	26
Oastler, Richard	64	Royal Infirmary	60
Oastler College of Education	64,73	Royal Institute of British Architects (RIBA)	passim
Oxford Extension Movement	33,34		
Paris Exhibition, 1867	16	Sadler, Sir Michael E.	29,30,31,32,33, 43,47,55
Parliamentary Committee on Scientific Instruction	16	St. Joseph's School	62,114
Patterson, Dr. J.	99	St. Paul's Church	57,60
Peat, Marwick, Mitchell & Co.	91	St Paul's Hall	112
Peel, Sir Robert	15	St Peter's Building	142
Percy, Lord Eustace	49	School Boards	26
Percy Report, 1945	49, 55	Schwann, Frederic	2,3,4,6,14,17,60
Phillips, George Searle	4, 5, 6, 7, 13	Science & Art Department	15,16,17
Philosophical Hall	3,4	Science and Engineering Research Council (SERC)	120,127
PICKUP Project	113,120		
Polytechnic Exhibition	4	Scott, Dr. W.E., MBE	55,56,57,58, 62,63
Polytechnic of Central London (PCL)	85,89,122	Second World War	48, 49
Polytechnic of Huddersfield Academic Credit Scheme	140	Sheard, K.	73,99
		Shiraz Project	90
Polytechnics & Colleges Admissions System (PCAS)	146	Sikes, Sir Charles W.	5
		Sisson, Ald. Douglas	75,85
Polytechnics & Colleges Funding Council (PCFC)	124,125,126,128, 136,137,138,139, 141,142,143,144, 145,146,147,148, 155	Smith, Cllr. Mrs Jessie	85
		Society for the Diffusion of Useful Knowledge	1
		Society of Arts	15,17
		Somerset, Duke of	19
Post Office Savings Bank	5	Sports Hall	61,120
Preliminary Savings Bank	5	Starkey Brothers, Messrs.	13
Prague : See Charles University		Starkey, Joseph, JP	14
Prince Consort	13	Steinitz, Richard	112
Privy Council	15,26,42,146	Storthes Hall Estate	144,148
Professoriate, establishment of	111	Student numbers	passim
'Pupil Teachers'	17	Students' Union	62,108,114,117, 120,128,141,142, 143,148
'Rag Week'	62		
Ramage, Dr. G.R.	63	President of	100,120,123,142, 143,144,148
Ramsden, Sir John William, Bart.	1,13,19,41		
Ramsden Building	35, n. 12	Sykes, Arthur	64
Ramsden Estate	18		
Ramsden Technical College	61	Taylor, Ken	62
		Teacher training	32

Technical and Evening Schools	33
Technical and Trade School	17
Technical Education in England and Wales (1889)	26
Technical Instruction Act, 1889	26,27
Technical Instruction Committees	26
Technical School and Mechanics' Institute (1884)	19
Temperance Hotel	2
Thatcher, Margaret H., Baroness	64
Thompson, J.	100
Thornhill family	4
Thorp, Thomas	27
Times Educational Supplement, The	55
Tittensor, Dr. Eric	74
Tolson, Legh T.	7,43
Tolson Memorial Museum	43
Tomlinson, George D.	7, 13
Topping, H.	41
Training Agency	127,137
Trippett, C.D.	92,122,123
Turner, Sir Joseph	41
Turpin, Dr. G.S.	26
Tylecote, Dr. Mabel	2
UCCA (Universities Admissions)	146
Universities' Funding Council (UFC)	144,145,146
University Council	146,147,148
University of Edinburgh	34
University Grants Committee (UGC)	55,56
University of Huddersfield	145,146
University of Leeds	19,28,30,32,34, 43,87
Van Kemenade, R.	121
Vice-Chancellor and Principal	146
Vice-Chancellor and Rector	146,148
Victoria University	28
Victoria University of Manchester	29
Ward, B	121,123
Welfare Committee	138
Wellington Buildings	5
West Riding County Council	27
'Whisky money'	26,27
White Paper:	
1943 : *Educational Reconstruction*	49
1956 : *Technical Education*	57,63
1961	58
1966 : *A Plan for Polytechnics and other Colleges*	58,59,61
1972	58
1987 : *Higher Education : Meeting the Challenge*	117
1991 : *Higher Education : A New Framework*	138,139,145
Whitaker, Dr. J.W., Principal	46,47,49,55
Willans, J.E.	7,50 n8
Willans, William	50n8
Wilson, James Harold, Baron Wilson	130 n.31
Wilson and Womersley, Architects	75
Wolfson Foundation	148
Woodhead, Dr. Thomas	31
Workers' Educational Association (WEA)	33,34
Wormald's Charity	18
Worshipful Company of Clothworkers	19
Yorkshire College	19
Yorkshire Council for Further Education (YCFE)	47,58
Yorkshire Union Board of Education	15,16,17
Yorkshire Union of Mechanics' Institutions	2,7,13